INSTRUCTIONAL SYSTEMS

Bela H. Banathy, Ed. D.

Fearon Publishers, Inc.

Belmont, California

To my wife, Eva

ISBN-0-8224-3950-6

Library of Congress Catalog Card Number: 68-31771

Printed in the United States of America.

Preface

In an age when problems seem to generate faster than we can identify them, and change appears to be the only certainty, we are eager to find ways to define and resolve our problems—complex as they are—and to cope with change, perpetual though it may be.

Evidence from various realms of our contemporary life indicates that in the systems concept we have available a way of thinking with which we can deal with complex problems and their changing relationships. In the systems approach we have a methodology, the use of which empowers us to develop and manage complex entities. In fact, we may have here something by which we can not only cope with our environment, but also be able to shape and master it and make change work for us.

Recognizing the potential power in systems theory and practice, educators have turned with increased interest toward the exploration of the systems concept and the use of the system approach. Although the educational application of the systems approach is still in the pioneering stage, many of us are encouraged by the results already achieved.

In this book I present recommendations for the use of the systems approach in designing curriculum. In curriculum construction there are variations in levels and complexities. There are also variations in levels of sophistication in the application of the systems approach. My intent is to discuss the use of simple system development strategies, on an introductory level, with those who are closest to the learner.

This book can be used in several different ways. It should enable the reader to understand the use of the systems approach in curriculum development. A productive competence can be attained if, in addition to reading the book, the user will *apply* the strategies described in designing materials on his own. The book can also be used in a course in curriculum construction or in in-service training programs.

I would like to express my gratitude to Dean James W. Brown of San Jose State, Professors Bentley T. Edwards and Robert M. Gagné of the University of California at Berkeley, and Dean Abraham S. Fishler of Nova University for their encouragement and helpful comments.

B. H. B.

Contents

Systems and Education 1

System is defined in the dictionary as *an assemblage of objects united by some form of regular interaction or interdependence; an organic or organized whole; as, the solar system; or a new telegraph system.* This definition suggests that there are differences in the kinds of systems. The solar system is a natural system; a telegraph system is designed by man. There are also hybrid systems which are combinations of natural and man-made systems—hydroelectric plants, for example, or modern dairies. In this book we will focus our attention on systems designed by man.

The dictionary definition is a good introduction to a discussion of systems. However, it is not a sufficient explanation of the rather special meaning of the term as it is used in this book. Although this special meaning is not in conflict with common usage, it is nevertheless different and rather specific. I will attempt here to explain the term by means of some examples.

The special meaning of the term *systems* and such related terms as *systems concept* and *systems approach* emerged during and after World War II as a result of research and development in problem solving, efficiency analysis, and, most significantly, the development of complex man-machine systems. In introducing a discussion of systems, writers usually refer to the design of weapons systems.[1] A classic example is the development of combat aircraft during World War II. In building such aircraft, designers realized that they could not simply take an existing airplane and add weapons, bomb and fuel storage space, communication and detection equipment, and protective armor. Adding such equipment at random restricted the plane's carrying capacity, speed, maneuverability, range of flight, and other vital functions. What emerged from this realization was a new method of planning and development in which designers learned that they first had to identify the purpose and performance expectations of the system before they could develop all the parts that made up the system as a whole. It is the system as a whole—and not its parts separately— that must be planned, designed, developed, installed, and managed. What is really significant is not how the individual components function separately, but the way they interact and are integrated into the system for the purpose of achieving the goal of the system. Generalizing from this example, *systems* can be defined as *deliberately designed synthetic organisms, comprised of interrelated and interacting components which are employed to function in an integrated*

[1] James D. Finn, "AV Development and the Concept of Systems," *Teaching Tools,* Vol. III, No. 4, Fall 1956.

fashion to attain predetermined purposes. Therefore, the best way to identify a system is to reveal its specific purpose.

Since World War II the developmental concept described here has been used with ever-increasing sophistication and it has rapidly expanded into new areas. Its military, industrial, and business applications are enormous. These include defense and communications systems, aerodynamics and space technology, industrial production, data retrieval and information processing, management and logistic systems, and numerous others.

Systems surround us everywhere. In the home, the housewife, the cooking equipment, the lighting, heating, water supply, storage and disposal facilities, the food, the dishes, and the cookbook all interact in a planned way to make up a meal-production system. Meal production is the purpose of the system. The stove, the refrigerator, the plumbing, lighting, and heating are components of the system. Their functions are determined by the purpose of the system, which is attained by the execution of processes in which components of the meal-production system engage in order to produce a predetermined outcome—edible food.

A further analysis suggests that the purpose of a system— in this case, meal production—determines the kinds of processes in which the system has to be engaged. In the case of a meal-production system, these processes will include planning the meals, acquiring, storing, preserving, and preparing the food, as well as sanitation and environmental control. These processes are further structured into subprocesses. For example, sanitation implies cleaning and disposal; the fancy term *environmental control* denotes the assignment of space and provision for heat, light, ventilation, and so on. The procedures that need to be carried out in order to achieve the purpose of the system will suggest the selection and employment of specific means or components. These components will be selected on the basis of their assessed capabilities in carrying out the processes. For example, food acquisition requires the introduction of such processes as financing, selecting sources of supply, purchasing, delivery, and so forth. The components employed in the process of selecting sources of supply may include the wife-husband team, other members of the family, friends, newspaper and mail advertisements, and such like. The process of delivery can be performed by members of the family with the family car, by a delivery man, by the milkman and his truck, or by some other means.

This example points out the three main aspects of systems—purpose, process, and content. The first aspect is that systems have *purpose*. Systems are built from parts or components, and the sum of these is the content of the system. The *content* of a system is organized for the accomplishment of a specific purpose. The operations and functions in which components are engaged in order to accomplish the purpose of the system add up to the *process* of the system. Going back to our example of aerospace systems, an airplane with other components, such as the flight and ground crew, airfield, weather report, and radar installations, communication and maintenance services, and so forth, may form the content of various systems, such as defense systems, transportation systems, or crop dusting and fire-fighting systems. The airplane, specifically designed for one of these systems, interacts with other components in the systems and jointly they engage in processes in order to attain the purpose for which they are built into the system.

Systems thus have purpose, process, and content. The sequence of purpose, process, and content is important because it implies priorities. Systems can be identified by their purpose. Purpose tells us what has to be done; it determines the processes that have to be undertaken. The content—the parts that comprise the system—is selected for its ability to accomplish the processes required in order to achieve the purpose of the system. The relationship of these three aspects is demonstrated in Figure 1.

Purpose gives direction to the whole system. It determines the processes that have to be generated in order to accomplish the purpose. The nature of the processes will

Figure 1

Aspects of the System

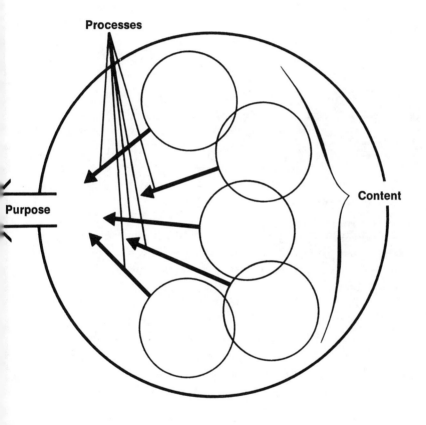

Processes

Purpose

Content

suggest the kinds of components that are to be employed and will make up the content of the system.

The relationship between purpose, process, and content is presented in Table A, in terms of a meal-production system.

An analysis of the information in Table A suggests that the planning, the acquisition of the food, the sanitation, and so on, can be viewed as subsystems that make up the meal-production system. Figure 2 illustrates this concept.

Subsystems

A subsystem is a part of a total system. Each subsystem is designed to carry out a purpose, the attainment of which is necessary in order to achieve the over-all purpose of the system. The processes of each subsystem are determined by the purpose of the subsystem; the components of each subsystem are selected on the basis of their abilities to carry out specific processes.

Subsystems operate in an integrated fashion. In a meal-production system, planning is integrated with and influenced by food acquisition, which then interacts with storage, preservation, preparation, and other subsystems. The effectiveness of the system depends on how well the subsystems are integrated and how well they interfunction.

There is a further hierarchal relationship that can be explored here. The meal-production system is in itself a subsystem of a larger system—the home. It is this *suprasystem,* the home, from which the meal-production system receives its purpose, resources, demands, and limitations.

Suprasystems

Systems operate in the larger context of their environment. This larger context can be conceived as the suprasystem of a particular system. For example, the larger context of education is society. Society is the suprasystem of education. Figure 3 depicts the relationship of education to society.

Table A

Relationships of Purpose, Process, and Content

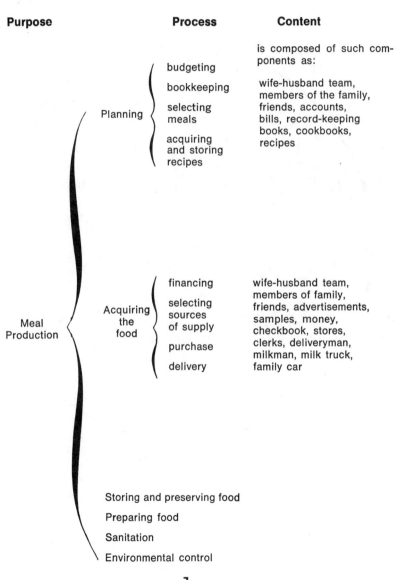

Purpose	Process	Content
		is composed of such components as:
	Planning { budgeting, bookkeeping, selecting meals, acquiring and storing recipes	wife-husband team, members of the family, friends, accounts, bills, record-keeping books, cookbooks, recipes
Meal Production	Acquiring the food { financing, selecting sources of supply, purchase, delivery	wife-husband team, members of family, friends, advertisements, samples, money, checkbook, stores, clerks, deliveryman, milkman, milk truck, family car
	Storing and preserving food	
	Preparing food	
	Sanitation	
	Environmental control	

Figure 2

System-Subsystem Relationship

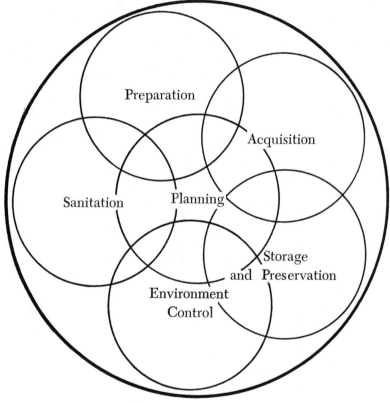

Meal Production System

Figure 3

A Suprasystem

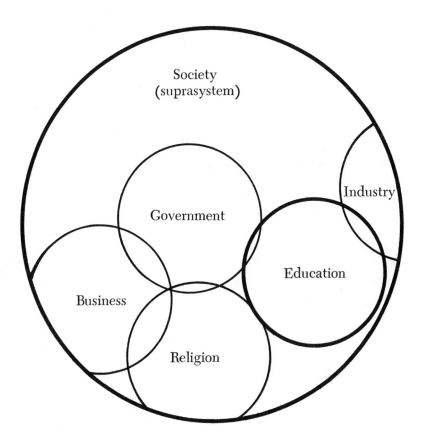

There are also other systems which are subsystems of society and which we call peer systems of education—for example, government, business, industry, and religion. The suprasystem has its own purpose, process, and content. The suprasystem surrounds the system and interacts with it. It is from the suprasystem that the system receives its input. From society, for example, education receives its purpose as well as its pupils, personnel, and material resources. It is into the suprasystem that the system sends its output. In the case of education, these outputs include the person who has been educated and the knowledge that has been developed. It is the environment—the suprasystem—that accepts or rejects the output of a system. Thus, if a system is to maintain itself, it is essential that it ensure the adequacy of its output. In order to ensure such adequacy, the system has to provide for a continuous assessment of its output and for a feedback of this assessment into the system. The feedback of the output assessment emerges as a basis for *system adjustment.* The structured relationship of input-output and feedback is shown in Figure 4, which depicts the first major adjustment demand that must be satisfied in order for the system to maintain compatibility with its environment.

There is also a second way in which a system must be able to adjust to its environment. The environment imposes constraints within which the system has to operate. The resources that are available to a system from its environment are usually limited and the system is therefore judged by its environment on the way it uses these resources.

Third, a system must be sensitive to the changing needs and purposes of its environment. A system is created by its environment for a purpose. The larger purpose of the environment influences or determines the purpose of its component systems. In other words, the system must be continuously aware of this larger purpose. It must be ready to adjust the purpose of the system if necessary, and, thus, the system itself. (However, the environment or the suprasystem is also influenced and affected by the outputs of its

Figure 4

Input-Output and Feedback Relationships

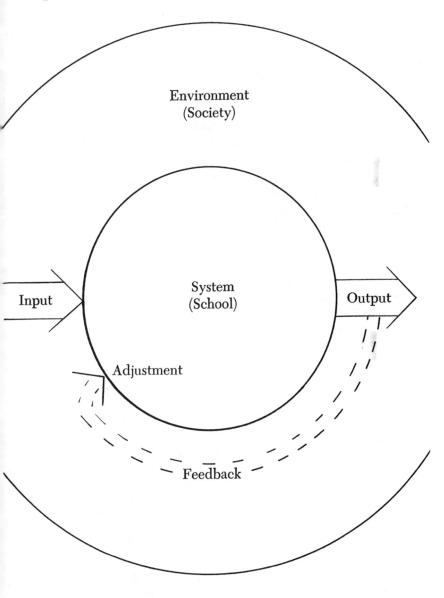

systems. For example, the learned person and the knowledge produced by the school will have much to do with bringing about changes in society.)

We are now ready for a comprehensive definition of the special meaning of the term *systems*. *Systems are assemblages of parts that are designed and built by man into organized wholes for the attainment of specific purposes. The purpose of a system is realized through processes in which interacting components of the system engage in order to produce a predetermined output. Purpose determines the process required, and the process will imply the kinds of components that will make up the system. A system receives its purpose, its input, its resources, and its constraints from its suprasystem. In order to maintain itself, a system has to produce an output which satisfies the suprasystem.*

Our goals are to learn to look at man-made entities in our environment as the kinds of systems defined here, and to integrate the systems concept into our own thinking. This special way of looking at the world requires us to search for specific purposes of entities and to relate functions and processes to the purposes of these entities. We are to search for cause-and-effect relationships, to recognize structures and relationships and look for ways of optimizing the interaction of components. The system outlook will require us to assess performance continuously, to exercise quality control and based on it to adjust and plan for improvement. This systems way of looking at things is called the *systems view*. The integration of this systems view into our own thinking will probably require many of us to break certain sets of thinking habits and acquire some new ones.

The systems view may call for some change in the way we usually conduct our inquiries. When we look at something or consider something, our usual sequence of inquiry is: What is it? What does it do? What is it for? Unfortunately, we often stop our inquiry as soon as we find an answer to the first question. When we discuss education, for example, most of us can give a rather precise description of schools, facilities, books, media, personnel, curriculums, and similar items. We become less specific, however, when it comes to describing what education does, and we are often shockingly vague when we attempt to explain what education is for.

Systems thinking *begins* by finding an answer to the question, What is it for? Indeed, it requires a rather detailed, specific definition of purpose. Only if we clearly identify purpose can we specify what has to be done, by what or by whom.

Systems thinking also requires us to pay more attention to the attainment of the purpose and consequently to the assessment of the attainment of the purpose of systems. When we look at a system with its purpose in mind, our central concern is with the optimum organization of the resources of the system in order to ensure the accomplishment of the performances required for the attainment of its stated purpose. Therefore, *the key criterion by which the effectiveness or adequacy of the performance of a system can be evaluated is how closely the output of the system satisfies the purpose for which it exists.*

Because a system is accountable for the use of the resources that have been made available to it, the economy of the system is another criterion by which the adequacy of a system can be assessed. The goal is to attain system objectives with the least possible effort and the least expenditure of time and resources.

Systems view can be characterized by a readiness to accept—and even more, to plan—for changes in a system. This readiness to change and be changed is a characteristic that many of us find difficult to acquire, but which, from the point of view of adequate systems operation, is most significant.

We have now reached the point where we can evolve a definition of the *systems approach.* Keeping in mind our special meaning of the word *systems,* and looking at manmade entities as implied by the systems view, *the systems approach appears to be the application of the systems view, or systems thinking, to human endeavors.*

The term *human endeavors* has been purposefully selected

to imply a wide range of applicability. An examination of the contemporary use of systems approach indicates at least three major areas of application. The example of the weapons system presented earlier has already introduced *systems development*. Systems development is the use of systems thinking in the design and development of synthetic entities. The systems approach, however, has been applied to at least two other areas—the analysis of the effectiveness and economy of existing systems, and the solution of complex problems. Often the terms *systems analysis* and *operations research* refer to these applications. The basic concept—the systems concept— underlies all three systems methodologies and there is a great deal of similarity in the strategies used by each of them. Still, there are enough differences among them to warrant separate treatment and explanation. By design the subject of this book has been limited to systems development. This limitation, however, does not imply that the educational application of systems analysis or operations research would be of lesser significance. In fact, systems analysis is being used with increasing frequency to evaluate the efficiency and effectiveness of educational systems, and operations research offers unique strategies for the solution of complex educational problems.

Our discussion has gradually unfolded a definition of systems, the systems concept, and systems view, and has arrived at a general desciption of the systems approach. This gradual unfolding is demonstrated in Figure 5.

The systems approach to the development of systems offers a decision-making structure and a set of decision-making strategies. It makes available for the designer a self-correcting, logical process for the planning, development, and implementation of man-made entities. It provides a procedural framework within which the purpose of the system is first specified and then analyzed in order to find the best way to achieve it. On the basis of this analysis, the components that are most suitable to the successful performance of the system can be selected. Next, systems planning will ensure that

Figure 5

From Systems to System Development

Note the feedback line. An understanding of the "systems nature" of synthetic entities enables us to build such entities as systems.

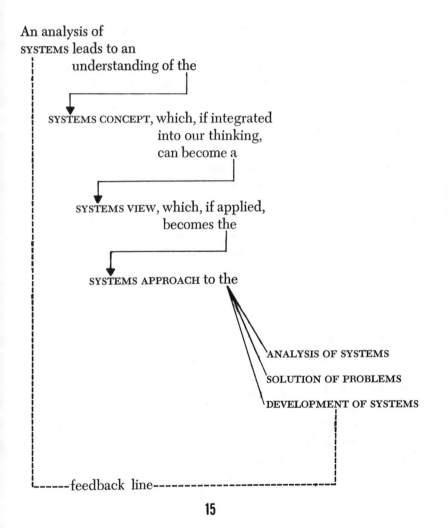

An analysis of
SYSTEMS leads to an
      understanding of the

SYSTEMS CONCEPT, which, if integrated
      into our thinking,
      can become a

SYSTEMS VIEW, which, if applied,
      becomes the

SYSTEMS APPROACH to the

ANALYSIS OF SYSTEMS

SOLUTION OF PROBLEMS

DEVELOPMENT OF SYSTEMS

└------feedback line---------------------------→--┘

appropriate components will be available at the proper time and will interact with other components as planned. Finally, continuous evaluation of the system oversees the implementation of the purpose and provides a basis for planned change in improving economy and performance.

The application of the systems approach to the development and maintenance of systems makes it possible to ensure that the performance specifications prescribed for the output of the system will be met. If they are not met, performance shortcomings can be assessed and the reasons for failing to meet the expected output performance can be identified. Then, appropriate adjustments can be made in the components and in the processes in order to achieve the desired output and optimize the effectiveness and economy of the system.

The success of the use of the systems approach has been clearly manifested in industry, business, and government. The systems approach is neither a new invention nor is it a miraculous discovery. It is rooted in such diversified fields as logic, philosophy, communication theory, psychology, and others. It is a pragmatic application of the scientific method; it is a synthesis of successful methodologies in problem solving, planning, and development, used by many people in many fields over a long period of time. Briefly, *the systems approach is common sense by design.*

Significance to Education

Systems analysis, systems approach, and *systems development* are high-frequency terms in educational circles. People, of course, respond to these terms in different ways. Some say that they are fads and will soon disappear. Some are convinced that these terms are just new words for things we have been doing all along. Others firmly believe that we can solve all our problems by the systems way. I profess to belong to a fourth category, one made up of those who are aware of the successful use of the systems approach in many areas of contemporary life and who, therefore, are interested in exploring its application to education.

I also believe that methods like or similar to the systems approach have been used and are being used by people in education even though not labeled as such. For some people, therefore, an exploration of the educational use of the systems approach may provide a framework for a synthesis of effective methods into a comprehensive methodology of planning and development.

In assessing the significance of the systems approach to education, we should first determine if education is really a system in the sense we are using the term. Education is certainly a man-made synthetic organism with a specific purpose. Its purpose is usually integrated with and influenced by the purpose of its suprasystem, society. It is society from which education receives its input, resources, constraints, and evaluation of adequacy. Education also has numerous subsystems such as the instructional subsystem, guidance, administration, and so on. Each of these subsystems has its own objective and yet each serves the over-all purpose. As the subsystems function, they influence the performance of their peer subsystems. Education is, furthermore, product oriented, its products being the educated man and the knowledge produced through research. Those responsible for conducting education also try to practice and promote economy. They attempt to maximize output, to improve continuously the performance of the product with the most economical use of resources. We can conclude, then, that education *is* a system in our specific sense of the term, and that education may therefore benefit from the application of the systems approach.

Realizing the systems nature of education and the unique potential that the systems approach can bring to the treatment of complex problems and the design of educational programs, it is no wonder that many educators have turned to the systems approach. As a result, the systems approach is already in use in numerous educational endeavors. (Projects and programs designed according to the systems concept include Alamitos School District, Garden Grove, California; Articulated Instructional Media Program at the University of Wisconsin; Center for Instructional Communication at Syracuse University; Instructional Systems Institute at Texas Christian University; Instructional Technology and Media Project, School of Education, University of Southern California; Learning Systems Institute and the Instructional Systems Development at Michigan State University; Project ULTRA at the N.Y. Institute of Technology; The Systems Approach to Instruction at Southern Connecticut State College; The Systems Approach in the Livonia School System and at Oakland Community College, both in Michigan. The Systems Development Corporation, under contract with the USOE, has just completed a two-and-one-half-year analysis of innovative instructional systems in five secondary schools in Alabama, Florida, Michigan, and Utah. Two major training programs are under way at Chapman College, Los Angeles, California, which are to prepare educators from California and other states for leadership in the systems approach to education. A recent conference, Project Aristotle, cosponsored by the Department of Defense, the U.S. Office of Education, and the National Security Industrial Association, clearly manifested the advanced use of the systems concept in education, industry, and the military.)

In spite of the rapidly increasing use of systems thinking in education, we should not assume, however, that in the systems approach we now have something solidly established that will ensure the solution of all our problems. First, the applications listed above should be looked upon as pioneering attempts. Furthermore, we should not expect that the system methodologies used in industry, business, and government are directly transferable to educational use. If anything, they should be *transformed* rather than transferred, as there is a need for their retooling.

Even though there is an impressive list of evidence of the educational use of the systems approach, the designer of an instructional system has only very limited reliable research data available to him and must therefore make pragmatic and intuitive design decisions. Surely a pragmatic point of view and intuition will always be useful to a systems designer; but we should demand—and continuously look for—research evidence. What is required, therefore, is a considerable amount of experimentation and testing in the educational applications of the systems approach.

Systems for Learning 2

The most conspicuous aspects for the systems approach are:

1. An insistence upon a clear definition of the purpose of the system, and upon the formulation of performance expectations stated specifically enough to enable the construction of criterion measures that will reveal evidence of the degree to which expected performance has been attained.
2. The examination of the characteristics of the input.

3. The consideration of alternatives and the identification of what has to be done and how, by whom or by what, when and where, so as to ensure that the predetermined performance will be attained.

4. The implementation of the system and the testing of its output for the purposes of measuring the degree to which performance expectations are being met and assessing the efficiency of systems operations.

5. The identification and implementation of any adjustments needed in order to ensure the attainment of the purpose and optimize system output and system economy.

Transforming these major system strategies into the domain of education will require us to:

1. Formulate specific learning objectives, clearly stating whatever the learner is expected to be able to do, know, and feel as an outcome of his learning experiences.

2. Develop tests to measure the degree to which the learner has attained the objectives.

3. Examine the input characteristics and capabilities of the learners.

4. Identify whatever has to be learned so that the learner will be able to perform as expected.

5. Consider alternatives from which to select learning content, learning experiences, components, and resources needed to achieve the stated objectives.

6. Install the system and collect information from the findings of performance testing and systems evaluation.

7. Regulate the system. The feedback from testing and evaluation will serve as a basis upon which the system will be changed—by design—in order to ensure ever-improving learning achievement and optimum systems economy.

A survey of the contemporary educational scene will lead us to realize the presence of some marked inadequacies in the strategies discussed above—namely, (1) in stating educational objectives, (2) in their testing and evaluation, (3) in the assessment of input competence, (4) in the implementation of objectives by a curriculum, (5) in evaluation, and (6) in the use of feedback for a continuous, built-in improvement of learning performance and systems operation. Let us discuss these inadequacies in more detail.

Statements of educational objectives set down by local school boards or found in state guidelines are usually stated in such general terms that they permit a broad interpretation of what the actual learning tasks are and of what content, learning experiences, and components are best suited to achieve them. Teachers are not usually accustomed to defining learning outcomes in operational and measurable terms. When they are asked about outcome expectations, most teachers will say something about finishing the book, or having their students earn good marks on exams. Without adequately specified objectives, it is difficult to assess input capabilities relevant to objectives. Information on student characteristics is seldom complete. Learning content is usually equated with textbooks and it is determined—at best —by the departmental committees that select the books. Without clearly identified learning objectives, textbook selection lacks relevance. Without clear-cut objectives those who select the books cannot really know what books are relevant. Vaguely stated objectives cannot serve as bases for designing output measures. As a result of these deficiencies, students are often unclear as to what is expected of them. They are sometimes tested on materials they have not learned, they are sometimes involved in studying subjects they have already mastered, or scheduled to master tasks which they are not given an opportunity to be assessed on. In contemporary instructional programs there is an obvious lack of clearly designed and well-integrated curriculums, a lack of internal congruence of objectives, curriculums, and testing. There are only few provisions, at best, for intentioned built-in improvement of the learning programs and the learner's performance.

Having joined the many who are always ready to say something about the shortcomings of education, I would now like to join the not so many who have something practical to offer in the way of improving existing conditions. To do this I intend first to identify the purpose or nucleus around which educational systems should be designed, and then present the design structure and systems strategies that can be applied in developing systems for learning.

The Nucleus Around Which Educational Systems Grow

In Chapter 1 it was noted that systems are developed around a purpose, as purpose is the nucleus around which a system grows. We must now ask, what is the purpose around which to build systems in education?

I believe we have a choice. We can say that the purpose of education is to *impart* specific knowledge, skills, and attitudes—in other words, the purpose around which the system is to grow is *instruction*. On the other hand, we can propose that the purpose of education is to ensure the attainment of specified knowledge, skills, and attitudes—thus, *learning* is the purpose around which the system is to grow.

In making a distinction here between instruction and learning, I don't believe that I am playing with words. For me this difference is crucial. In this book I plan to demonstrate what I mean by an educational system that has learning as its nucleus. Although my aim here is not to explain the difference between learning and instruction, I would still like to mention a few points that indicate the significance of a difference.

First, the typical classroom sets up an environment and a classroom procedure in which one person (the teacher) faces 30 or 40 students. The environment is uniform and regulated for all, and the processes are instruction and control. If, on the other hand, learning were in focus, no one would seriously suggest such a setup, as it is obvious that 30 or 40 persons cannot learn in the same way. Second, we find that 40 or 50 minutes is the amount of time usually scheduled for one class period. If learning were in focus, such rigid scheduling would not exist, inasmuch as we know that people learn at different rates of speed, and therefore need different amounts of time to master a particular learning task. In the setup described above, the teacher's role is to be the main source of information; he is to impart knowledge; he is the main actor and the students are his audience. In a learning-oriented system, the roles would change. The learner would be on stage and do the acting, and the teacher would manage the learning. To mention another contrast, today we talk about audiovisuals as aids to teaching and books in the library as supplements to instruction. In the systems view, on the other hand, if the capability of a certain medium or library resource indicates that it is the best component to facilitate learning then it would be used—not as an aid or supplement, but as the component selected on the basis of its measured potential to bring about the desired learning.

Some recent statements seem to support the distinctions made here. Hedegard[1] juxtaposed two kinds of educational systems. In the first, the learner's role is "reacting" while the teacher's role is "active." The teacher selects content and learning experiences and the learner reacts to them. The teacher's thought processes involve organization, while the student only reacts by making passive connections of impressions. The learner's unique motives are rarely accepted, often discouraged, and sometimes even punished. In the second system, the learner assumes an active role in selecting content and learning experiences. His thought processes involve organization. He is required to do more than passively connect impressions. In the learning environment, experiences are sought that are personally satisfying to the learner. Rogers[2] reports on an instruction-focused approach accord-

---

[1] James M. Hedegard, "An Overview of Historical Formulations." In *Instruction: Some Contemporary Viewpoints*, Lawrence Siegel (ed.), (San Francisco: Chandler Publishing Co., 1967).

[2] Carl R. Rogers, "The Facilitation of Significant Learning." Ibid.

ing to which (1) the student is usually not trusted to pursue his own learning, (2) presentation is believed to equal learning and whatever was covered in class has therefore been learned by the student, (3) only what is considered to be established knowledge is dealt with, (4) the student learns passively, and (5) the student must give an account of his progress at regularly scheduled examinations, the passing of which is the all-important goal.

In designing curriculums, it is learning which should be in focus; systems in education should be built for one purpose: learning. I do not intend to degrade the value of instruction, but I do want to suggest that it should be viewed in its proper relationship to learning and treated accordingly.

On the basis of this discussion, I suggest that instruction is the *process* rather than the *purpose* of education. In the systems view, instruction denotes processes and functions that are introduced into the environment of the learner in order to facilitate the mastering of specific learning tasks. Accordingly, any interaction between the learner and his environment through which the learner is making progress toward the attainment of specific and purposed knowledge, skills, and attitudes is viewed as instruction.

The effectiveness of an instructional system, therefore, can be measured by assessing the degree to which it provides for the learner a system for learning. An instructional system serves its purpose to the extent to which it brings about in the environment of the learner all the possible interactions that result in the attainment of the desired performance. It is, I believe, through the line of reasoning developed here that instruction can become fully compatible with learning. It is by this rationale that the title *Instructional Systems* was selected for this book.

The Structure of the Developmental Design

The development of a system for learning is a decision-making operation. Decisions have to be made about what should be learned, how, by whom, when, and where; how

Figure 6

An Overview of Structure

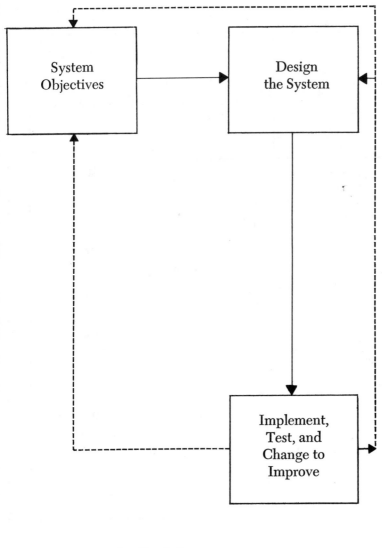

------------------ feedback line

Figure 7

An Over-all Structure of the Design of an Instructional System

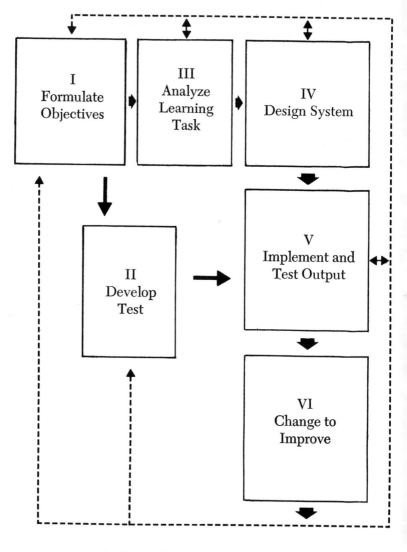

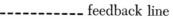 feedback line

learning should be evaluated and improved, and what resources should be involved in preparing for, providing for, and evaluating learning. The systems approach to design and development offers a logical structure and the orderly use of strategies for making these curriculum decisions. It is my intent to introduce this structure and describe the systems strategies that can be used in the development of instructional systems. See Figures 6 and 7.

The decision-making structure shown in Figure 6 provides for the orderly development and change of the system. The objectives of the system will determine whatever has to be designed and done to attain system objectives. The design is then implemented and the output tested by criterion measures developed on the basis of objective specifications. The test findings are interpreted in order to measure the extent to which the objectives have been reached. If necessary, the system can be redesigned in order to ensure the accomplishment of its objectives.

Let us now consider the structure described in Figure 6 and apply it to the design of instructional systems. At the same time let us try to be a little more specific than we have been so far.

I. The initial step is to formulate a statement that spells out what we expect the learner to do, know, and feel as a result of his learning experiences (Formulate Objectives).

II. Develop a criterion test based on objectives and use it to test terminal proficiency (Develop Test).

III. Find out what has to be learned by the student so that he can behave in the way described by the objectives specifications. In the course of this analysis, the input capabilities of the learner must also be assessed—he does not have to learn whatever he already knows (Analysis of Learning Task).

IV. Consider alternatives and identify what has to be done to ensure that the learner will master the tasks (Functions Analysis). Determine who or what has the best potential to accomplish these functions (Component Analysis). Decide when and where the functions are to be carried out (Design of the System).

V. The designed system can now be tried out or tested, implemented, and installed. The performance of the learner, who is the product of the system, is to be evaluated in order to assess the degree to which he behaves in the way initially described (Implement and Test Output).

VI. Findings of the evaluation are then fed back into the system to see what changes—if any—are needed to improve the system (Change to Improve).

We have now reached the point, within the broad framework presented above, where we can proceed to identify and discuss the component strategies of the development and design of instructional systems.

The Formulation of Objectives 3

The process of formulating objectives is viewed as a gradually unfolding specification, refinement, and description of the expected output performance of the learner. First, the over-all purpose of the system must be identified. In a statement of purpose we need to identify the goal that the learner is to attain. Once the purpose or goal has been determined, performance objectives can be derived and described as specifically as it is possible and feasible. The strategies that comprise the formulation of objectives will be discussed next.

31

System Purpose

An educational system can be best identified by its purpose. A statement of purpose will establish the nucleus around which the system should grow. In general terms the statement tells us the reason for the system's existence. This statement should also reveal some key information about the system as a whole. It should briefly tell us about the environment of the system and about some of the broad constraints under which the system is to operate. The adjective *broad* is significant in that specific constraints will be considered only during the design phase of the development of the system.

To illustrate, let us see how a statement of purpose can be formulated for a course entitled "The Application of the Systems Approach." The purpose of this course is to introduce the application of the systems approach to the development of systems for learning. As an output, the student is expected to construct a system in a subject area of his own choosing. More specifically, the course aims to:

> Develop an understanding of the systems concept and evolve a systems view for the purpose of designing educational curriculums.
>
> Assist participants in selecting a purpose around which to build their systems.
>
> Demonstrate to participants the potential and the strategy of the systems approach in designing systems.
>
> Guide participants in the actual application of the systems approach to their selected project.
>
> Provide opportunities to participants to enable them to demonstrate their competence in the use of the systems approach.

The following statement describes the environment of the course and some of its over-all constraints:

> This course is offered in extension, in the working environment of participants—such as teachers, curriculum workers, and administrative personnel—who most likely will take this course as part of their professional development program. A professional level course in education, the course is managed by an instructor in fifteen three-hour sessions. Only limited library facilities are available.

A statement of purpose, however, is not a statement of objectives, although it is the point of departure in formulating objectives.

Specification of Objectives

The systems approach confronts us with specific requirements as to how the objectives should be stated. In evolving these requirements, I have found the statements of Mager,[1] Tyler,[2] Smith,[3,4] and Gagné[5,6] most useful.

Objectives are to be deduced from the purpose of the system. A statement of objectives should specify:

1. *What* the learner is expected to be able to do, by
   a. Using verbs that denote observable action.
   b. Indicating the stimulus that is to evoke the behavior of the learner.
   c. Specifying resources (objects) to be used by the learner and persons with whom the learner should interact.
2. *How well* the behavior is expected to be performed by identifying
   a. Accuracy or correctness of response.
   b. Response length, speed, rate, and so forth.
3. *Under what circumstances* the learner is expected to perform by specifying

[1]Robert F. Mager, *Preparing Instructional Objectives* (Palo Alto, Calif.: Fearon Publishers, 1962).

[2]Ralph W. Tyler, "Some Persistent Questions on the Defining of Objectives." In *Defining Educational Objectives,* C. M. Lindvall (ed.), (Pittsburgh: University of Pittsburgh Press, 1964).

[3]Robert G. Smith, Jr., *The Development of Training Objectives.* Research Bulletin 11 (Alexandria, Va.: HumRRO, 1964).

[4]Robert G. Smith, Jr., *The Design of Instructional Systems.* Technical Report 66-18 (Alexandria, Va.: HumRRO, 1966).

[5]Robert M. Gagné, *The Conditions of Learning* (New York: Holt, Rinehart and Winston, 1965).

[6]Robert M. Gagné, "Educational Objectives and Human Performance." In *Learning and the Educational Process,* J. D. Krumboltz (ed.), (Chicago: Rand McNally, 1965).

    a. Physical or situational circumstances.
    b. Psychological conditions.

If the objective is formulated in this way, its attainment will be measurable and it can also serve as a basis for the development of the system. The following example demonstrates the formulation of objectives derived from one of the purposes of the course in "The Application of the Systems Approach."

Objectives for Demonstrating Competence in the Use of the Systems Approach to the Development of a Micro-System[7]

Applying the strategy of the systems approach, participants of this course will be able to develop, install, and evaluate a micro-system of their choice. It is expected that consumers of this micro-system will attain predetermined objectives or, if not, the designer of the system will be able to adjust his system so that the objective will be eventually attained. Participants in this course will be asked to demonstrate the capability described above by submitting a typewritten description of the micro-system they developed, noting both the process of development, installation, evaluation, and change, and the products of the developmental effort.

Let us now evaluate this objective. Does it meet the specifications that we have described in the paragraph above?

1. *How does this objective describe* what *is expected?*
    a. Does it use verbs denoting observable action?
       It says, "Submit a typewritten description of the micro-system they developed, noting both the process . . . and the products . . ."
    b. Does it indicate the stimulus that is to evoke the expected behavior?
       Yes, two kinds of stimulus are indicated: (1) *"applying the*

[7]A *micro-system* is viewed here as the smallest unit of curriculum in which, however, all characteristics of curriculum are still reflected. It is developed around a clearly defined objective, the mastering of at least one learning task is required and alternatives can be considered for content, learning experiences, motivation, and for the selection of components. Furthermore, it can be installed and tested as a unit.

strategy of the systems approach . . ." and "participants in this course *will be asked to demonstrate their capability . . . by submitting . . .*"

   c. Does it specify resources to be used and the persons to interact?
     This aspect is implied by the notion that testing the system will require the involvement of students; the description of the system will require the use of a typewriter.

2. *How does the objective state* how well *the behavior is expected to be performed?*
   There are two clues indicating performance expectations:
   a. "It is expected that consumers of this micro-system will attain predetermined objectives or, if not, the designer of the system will be able to adjust his system so that the objective will be eventually attained."
   b. "Submit a description of the micro-system they develop, noting both the process of development, installation, evaluation, and change, and the products of the developmental effort."

3. *How does the objective state the circumstances under which the learner is expected to perform?*
   There are again two clues:
   a. The designer is expected to install his system; this implies operation in an instructional environment.
   b. Submit a typewritten statement; this implies that the criterion behavior will be demonstrated at the convenience of the participant, probably by developing this written report in his home environment.

Our analysis of the sample objective indicates that the criterion suggested for the formulation of objectives was indeed applied. But is this objective, in the form stated, specific enough? In formulating objectives, the designer should strive for a continuous refinement of objectives. We will now consider how far this refinement should go, or how specific an objective should be.

By continually refining his objectives, the designer should arrive at a level of specificity which reaches down to the individual task level.[8] The example that follows demonstrates

---

[8] Gagné defines this task level as ". . . the smallest unit of performance which can be identified as having a distinct and independent purpose." Robert M. Gagné, "Educational Objectives and Human Performance." *Op.cit.,* p. 12.

a further, task-level refinement of the objective we have just evaluated.

Participants of this course will be asked to demonstrate the capability described above by submitting a typewritten description of the micro-system they developed, noting both the process of development, installation, evaluation and change, and the products of the developmental effort.

This objective can be further specified on the task level:

Participants are expected to submit:

A. A statement of purpose of the selected system which is to be an over-all description of the system denoting the main anticipated learning environment, and constraints.

B. Descriptions of processes and products of the planning and development of the micro-system. The descriptions should include all of the following items.

1. A statement of objectives. This statement should specify what the learner is expected to be able to know, do, and feel as an outcome of his learning experiences. It should also specify how well the learner is expected to perform and under what circumstances. In writing this description (a) note the class of expected behavior, (b) use verbs that denote observable action, and (c) describe the stimuli that are to bring about such action. The expected behavior should be specified in terms of the smallest independent unit of performance.

2. A description of the test used for the assessment of student performance at the output point. This test is also used for the quality control of the system.

3. An inventory of learning. This is the result of an analysis of learning tasks. Based on a description of performance tasks, the analysis identifies whatever the individual has to learn in order to perform in the expected way.

4. A statement of expected input competence, which is an assessment of capabilities of the learner in relationship to the inventory of learning tasks.

5. A description of the test by which the input competences will be measured.

6. A statement of actual learning tasks which is evolved by computing the difference between the inventory of learning and whatever is assumed to be known by the learner at the input point.

7. The characterization of learning tasks. Identify the type of learning the learning task represents and estimate learning difficulty.

8. A presentation of the learning structure which is the product of the hierarchal arrangement of learning tasks. This arrangement is guided by an inquiry into a logical sequence; that is, the attainment of task A is a prerequisite to the learning of task B and so on.

9. An identification of functions, the accomplishment of which provides for the acquisition of specified learning tasks and thus for the achievement of stated objectives. This identification is the outcome of functions analyses. Consider at least the following functions: (a) Selection and organization of content. (b) Selection and organization of learning experiences. (c) Management of learning. (d) Ensuring learning. (e) Continuous evaluation of the system and the progress of the learner. Describe plans for carrying out selected functions. Consider the alternatives and give your rationale for selection of particular alternatives.

10. A description of the survey of components. Consider all feasible components—human, media, and other material resources—which have the potential to carry out functions. Give your rationale for distributing functions among components.

11. A schedule of what functions will take place, when and where they will be conducted, and by whom.

12. A description of plans and procedures for the preparation of instructional materials, for system training, and system testing.

13. Report on how the system was installed.

14. A report on the results of testing the students, together with the identification of changes, if any, which are planned to alter and improve the system, as based on the findings of the output testing.

The description of the products and processes of the development of the micro-system, implied by the above criteria, is to be prepared as a course project and it should be submitted not later than the session before the last.

Our second example is from another subject field. It demonstrates the formulation of objectives in foreign language education.

A System for the Acquisition of a Foreign Language

Purpose: Designed for adult, native speakers of English, the course has the purpose of leading toward the limited competence needed to get by in the most frequent and basic situations in which one finds himself in a foreign country.

The statement of objectives for this language course may have six parts: comprehension, speaking, reading, writing, cultural behavior, and cultural and area information. Of the six, I will consider here only speaking.

Objective for Speaking a Foreign Language

At the end of the course the learner will be able to speak the target language in communication events by speaking (a) to a native speaker of the language, or (b) to a person who has a better command of the language than he has.

The contexts in which the learner is expected to speak the target language are to be typical to the learner's everyday live communication events dealing with situations in which the learner would find himself as a visitor in the target country, such as communicating while in travel, short-contact social settings that are routine to a foreign visitor, and while engaging in conversations about events in which he has been involved.

In speaking the target language, the learner will be expected to (1) use kernel sentences and interrogative and negative transformations, (2) use out of alternative or optional forms only the most simple and those closest to his native language, (3) speak with a pronunciation permitting the transfer of only specifically identified sound features from the native language of the speaker, (4) exhibit a speed and fluency which, although less than that of the native, will still present the utterances spoken in sentence units, and (5) have a productive control of about 800 lexical items.

The learner will be able to perform such tasks as

1. Answering questions in reference to concrete phenomena immediately observable in the environment.
2. Asking questions about the same.
3. Describing a picture or object.
4. Describing his actions or the actions of those around him.
5. Repeating a short story he has just heard or read.
6. Engaging in a conversation about events in which he has been involved.
7. Communicating while traveling and in social situations that are routine to a foreign visitor.

An examination of these two examples will lead us to a recognition of a difference. In the first example the tasks listed are component tasks of the objective. The performance of *all* of the tasks is required for the demonstration of the expected behavior. The tasks listed in the foreign language example, on the other hand, are representative tasks. A demonstration of competence in one or two of them may be adequate proof of the attainment of terminal expectations.

Reviewing the objective samples presented in this chapter, we can recognize the tendency to be very specific in stating the expected outcome of learning. But why should we be so concerned about this? There are at least three reasons why we should insist on being quite specific in formulating objectives. First, a description of terminal performance becomes a basis upon which to construct the criterion test. The criterion test is the measuring instrument that is used to assess the degree to which the objective has been achieved. It will be the key means to the quality control of the system. Hence we say objectives should be stated in measurable terms. The second reason is that objectives should be stated in operational terms. This means that objectives should be stated in sufficient detail to be used as bases of departure for the actual development of the system they describe. The third reason is that objectives should be formulated in such a way that they will communicate clearly and unmistakably what we are trying to achieve to all who are involved in the system— primarily to the learner and the teacher, but also to any others who have a function in or an influence on the system.

Taking another look at our objective samples, we can make some further generalizations. The processes involved in stating the purpose of the system, in deriving objectives from the purpose and specifying objectives, appear to be of two kinds: analysis and synthesis. Having stated the over-all purpose of the system, we subjected it to an analysis in order to arrive at operational and measurable descriptions of objectives. A further analysis led us to refine objectives on the task level. The formulation of objectives, however, also included synthesis, inasmuch as they had to be constructed according to predetermined criteria. In designing systems, these two processes are often used in a complementary way, sometimes even simultaneously. However, the nature of the initial strategies of systems development consists more of analysis and that of subsequent strategies, as we will demonstrate later on, consists more of synthesis.

The Analysis of Learning Tasks 4

Once the specific performance expected of the learner has been identified, we can consider what he has to learn in order to be able to perform successfully. The next step, then, is for the system designer to analyze and formulate the learning tasks. The analysis and formulation of learning tasks is a procedure having a structure specific to it and it is composed of a set of strategies. Figure 8 presents this structure and identifies its component strategies.

Figure 8

The Analysis and Formulation of Learning Tasks

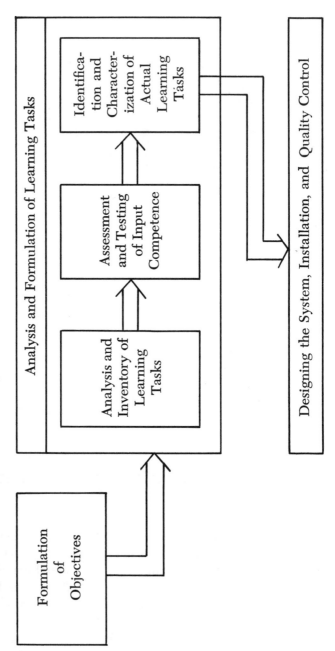

In this chapter I will describe the strategies identified in Figure 8 and will demonstrate their application. The first strategy is the analysis and inventory of learning tasks.

The Analysis and Inventory of Learning Tasks[1]

If we know from a statement of objectives the particular terminal performance expected of a student, we must then ask ourselves what does the student have to learn so that he can perform in the expected way? In other words, we must determine the human capabilities—skills, knowledge, and attitudes—that the individual needs to have in order to carry out the specified output performance.

It is important that we understand the difference between performance tasks and learning tasks. Performance tasks, as described in a statement of objectives, communicate to us behavior which the product of the system is expected to be able to exhibit at the output point. Learning tasks and their analysis identify whatever learning is to be undertaken by the learner to enable him to demonstrate the performance described.

The need to conduct an analysis of learning tasks is questioned by some. If an objective is stated specifically enough, doesn't it inform us as to what has to be learned? If the expected performance is described on behavioral terms, doesn't it also describe the learning task? The answer to these questions is not necessarily negative. It may well be that for certain categories of behavior, a description of output performance may also identify the learning tasks. This could be the case when the process of the acquisition of certain be-

---

[1]The process implied by the phrase "the analysis of learning task" is different from that denoted by "task analysis." Task analysis, as the term is commonly used, involves a detailed listing of component behavioral elements of a job or task and their interrelationships. For further reference, see Robert B. Miller, "Task Description and Analysis." In *Psychological Principles in System Development*, Robert M. Gagné (ed.), (New York: Holt, Rinehart and Winston, 1962).

havior falls into such categories as response and chain learning.[2] More specifically, whenever the attainment of a performance task requires only imitative behavior, we can say with some confidence that a statement of the task may also imply the learning task. Learning to open a lock by observing someone else do it or memorizing an utterance as a verbal chain may fall into this category. Even for these tasks, however, there is a need to "learn" to want to do them.

Most of the performance we want to facilitate in school, however, is within the cognitive and affective domains. Some of the types of learning involved here are multiple discrimination, perception and use of concepts and principles, problem solving, and decision making. A description of performance expectation in these domains will rarely, if ever, suffice as identification of learning tasks. Although it may be implied, a learning task is not explicit in a statement of performance. It must be uncovered, deduced by an examination and analysis of the task itself. The following examples demonstrate the analysis of learning tasks. We will develop first an analysis of learning tasks based on the objective of the language learning program discussed on page 38 in Chapter 3.

The learner will be able to perform such tasks as
1. Answering questions in reference to concrete phenomena immediately observable in the environment.
2. Asking questions about the same.
3. Describing a picture or object.
4. Describing his actions or the actions of those around him.
5. Repeating a short story he has just heard or read.
6. Engaging in a conversation about events in which he has been involved.
7. Communicating while traveling and in social situations that are routine to a foreign visitor.

An analysis of learning tasks commences by considering what has to be learned by the student so that he will be able to communicate in the situations described and with the accuracy specified. The learning task, of course, is not to

[2]Robert M. Gagné, *The Conditions of Learning* (New York: Holt, Rinehart and Winston, 1965).

memorize utterances that may be used in communication events under the circumstances described in the objective. Underlying even a brief utterance is a complex set of patterns operating in the various psychomotor, cognitive, and effective domains of communication behavior. The learning task in foreign language acquisition is to learn to perceive and use these patterns and, thus, to learn to generate novel utterances appropriate to the specific referential, situational, and cultural contexts in which the individual participates. Only a scientific analysis of the subject language and culture will be able to uncover all these patterns. The different kinds of patterns emerging from such analysis would suggest the establishment of the different categories of an inventory of learning tasks. One of these categories could cover sound features, intonation, and stress patterns. Another one could list sentence patterns the learner has to be able to use in order to speak in the manner implied by the objective.

The designer should include in the inventory specific paralanguage features and kinesics. Furthermore, the analysis must identify typical situations that are representative of the circumstances indicated in the statement of objectives and in the description of performance tasks. The analysis must also refer to categories of vocabulary that are related to the specified situations. The items uncovered by this analysis can be listed and arranged in an inventory. The information in this inventory will then serve as input data for the design and development of the system.

Up to now, the examples provided to demonstrate the use of the strategies of systems development have applied to learning on college and adult levels. Our next example concerns the analysis and inventory of learning tasks on the kindergarten level. The project[3] attempted to develop a guidance subsystem for parents of children entering kindergarten. The purpose of this subsystem was to assist parents to prepare their child for his new public school experience.

Of the numerous areas of development, social interaction

---

[3]Conducted at the Pacific Grove, California, School System in 1967.

was explored in depth. A whole set of objectives was formulated of which only one will be presented here as an example.

> In a kindergarten class, under the direction of the teacher, having heard a recorded story at a listening post, a child within a group of six to eight children will participate in discussing a story with his peers.
>
> Expectation: Within a four-week period, an increase of frequency of verbalization will be considered growth.

This objective was subjected to an analysis. The outcome of the analysis as reported here is not inclusive at all. It gives only hints of the types of learning tasks that a complete analysis would eventually uncover.

It is obvious that the child has to learn to converse on a given topic. But what does the child have to learn specifically in order to be able to do this?

Our analysis suggests that he has to learn to

1. Comprehend what has been communicated to him; to grasp significant elements and relationships.
2. Recall the story, its significant elements and relationships; recall events in chronological order.
3. Organize his verbal account of the story with authenticity (significant elements, relationships, order, and so on).

In order to do these things, he also has to learn to

1. Use patterns of language commonly used in the classroom.
2. Use words within their common range of meaning.

In addition, he must learn to

1. Understand that there are activities in which he is expected to participate.
2. Pay attention to what is being said.
3. Respond to certain verbal and nonverbal cues.
4. Wait for his turn.

This analysis demonstrates that a description of expected output behavior is only a basis for an analysis of learning tasks and it is not in itself a description of them. As a result of an inquiry of what has to be learned in order for the learner to be able to behave in the way described in the performance tasks, an inventory of learning tasks can be formulated. This inventory, however, will contain—most likely—more than what actually has to be learned. We will explore this notion next.

Input Competence

In most instances—probably in all instances—we will find that the learner brings to the learning situation some skills, information, attitudes, and so on, that are relevant to what he is supposed to learn. It would be a waste of time to teach competences that the learner already possesses. We usually refer to competences that are relevant as the *initial* or *input capabilities* of the learner.

In our kindergarten example, for instance, relevant to the child's verbal interaction with the teacher, it can be reasonably expected that the children will have experienced a range of verbal interaction with adult members of their families and other adults in their environment. The intensity of these experiences may vary from little or no participation to extensive participation in such things as dinner table discussion, church school experiences, family council, nursery school participation, or visits to the doctor's office.

It is the job of the system designer to assess the capabilities the student has already acquired relative to the learning inventory. This assessment is pertinent even in a case where the learner is to acquire some esoteric knowledge, such as a foreign language he has never heard of. The learner of the foreign language will have at his disposal at the input point features of his native language that are transferable into the target language. For example, native speakers of English who learn Spanish will find that certain syntactical constructions and some grammatical elements such as adverbs, prepositions, and conjunctions work in similar fashion in both languages. The concept of plurality exists in both languages; in fact, in both languages one of the ways to form plurals is by adding an *s* to a noun. There are also sounds in the phonological inventory of English that are transferable.

Input Test

By using an input test we can determine what a student already knows about a subject. Of course, this will vary from one student to another. To consider this variation is highly important. If we do not pay attention to individual differences in input capabilities, we invite trouble. The learner who has not acquired the capabilities we believe he should have will be frustrated and will probably fail. On the other hand, the student who is scheduled to learn something he already knows is going to be bored and will probably lose interest. A test of input capabilities will help to avoid both pitfalls. It will make it possible to provide a pre-input program to overcome deficiencies in some students and to arrange for the advanced placement of others.

The Identification and Characterization of Learning Tasks

It has already been mentioned that in most cases we will find that the learner has already acquired capabilities relevant to a particular set of learning tasks. The way to identify the actual task of learning is to subtract whatever is already known to the learner (input competence) from a specific set of learning tasks (inventory of learning tasks). See Figure 9.

For example, in learning to tell time in a foreign language, we will list in the inventory of learning tasks the ability to properly identify numbers as represented by the figures from 1 to 12. It will be expected, however, that this capability will be possessed by the child as an input competence. This capability, therefore, will not be identified as an actual learning task.

The characterization of learning tasks provides additional information about learning tasks. This information will be used as input data for the design of the system. There are

Figure 9

Computing the Actual Learning Tasks

Inventory of Learning Tasks

Minus

Input Competence

Equals

Actual Learning Tasks

two ways that this characterization can be accomplished. One is to specify the type of learning the acquisition of a particular learning task represents. Gagné[4] identifies a whole set of learning types, such as signal learning, response learning, motor and verbal chains, multiple discrimination, concept learning, principle learning, and problem solving. These types differ significantly as to the particular conditions which need to prevail in order to ensure the mastering of learning tasks for different types. For example, producing a new foreign language sound is identified as a response learning, the learning of "copying" a sound. The conditions governing this learning are very much different from the learning of the use of a new sentence structure, which is a principle learning. The use of a grammatical structure cannot be learned by copying or memorizing sentences in which the structure occurs.

The identification of the type of learning a learning task represents is indeed a most useful information. As we will explain later, this identification is one of the bases upon which to select and organize learning content and learning experiences.

The other dimension of learning-task characterization is quantification.[5] By quantification we mean an estimate or measure of the amount of difficulty the mastering of a specific learning task represents. This information is needed for two purposes. First, it can be used to project the time needed to hurdle a learning task, and second, it guides in making an estimate of the amount of content needed for the treatment of any particular learning task. Quantification data can be accrued from observing learning over a period of time and recording information relevant to the time needed for mastering the learning tasks.

As for an example, such quantification can be made by observing the pronunciation errors the learner makes and by

[4] Robert M. Gagné, *op. cit.*

[5] Bela H. Banathy, A *Theory of Selection and Organization of Content in Foreign Language Curricula.* Doctoral Dissertation (Berkeley, Calif.: University of California).

watching out for the persistence of these errors over a span of time. The more an error persists, the more attention, content, and time need to be devoted to the particular task.

A Review of Strategies and an Examination of Their Nature

The analysis and formulation of learning tasks lead the system designer to a point where he can clearly state what has to be learned in the system in general and by specific students in particular. The information in Figure 10 briefly reviews the strategies involved in this process. It also accounts for preceding strategies.

The data gained from the formulation of objectives serves as bases from which to proceed with a query of what has to be learned in order to attain the objectives of the system. As a result of this inquiry, an inventory of learning tasks is evolved. This inventory is then subjected to further analysis. In most cases we find that the learner has previously acquired some of the tasks listed in the inventory. The actual learning task is the residue of learning task inventory minus relevant input competence. Once the designer has identified the actual learning tasks, he must characterize them as to the type of learning they represent and as to the degree of difficulty they pose for the learner.

The nature of the processes employed during the strategies described up to this point is primarily analysis, but at times it is also synthesis. To begin with, an analysis of systems purposes leads to gathering data from which, through further analysis, a statement of objectives can be developed. The objectives must then be further analyzed in order to identify whatever the learner has to learn in order for him to behave in the way prescribed. This analysis provides the learning inventory. To assess input competence, a test relevant to the learning inventory must be constructed. Differential analysis of learning inventory versus input competence furnishes a set of actual learning tasks that can be characterized as to

Figure 10

Strategies of Analysis of Learning Tasks

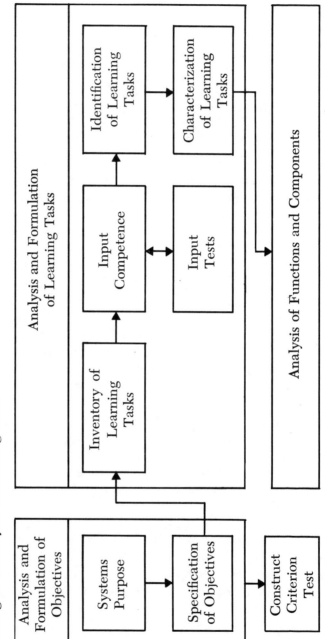

the kind of learning they represent and degree of difficulty they pose for the learner. Again, the integrated use of analysis and synthesis appears to be characteristic of these strategies.

This integrated process becomes further activated as system planning moves into the actual design of the system. The structure and strategies of this phase of systems development will be discussed in the next chapter.

The Design of the System 5

Once we have identified and characterized the tasks the learner is to attain, we can proceed with the design of a system that will provide for the mastering of these tasks. The following inquiries will guide the development of the design:

1. What has to be done to enable the learner to master the task?
2. Who or what has the capability of doing whatever has to be done?
3. Who or what will do exactly what?
4. When and where will they do it?

Consequently this third phase of systems development will consist of four major strategies:

1. Functions analysis (what has to be done and how).
2. Components analysis (who or what has the potential to do it).
3. Distribution of functions among components (who or what will do exactly what).
4. Scheduling (when and where it will be done).

Figure 11 illustrates the relationship of these strategies within the framework of the larger systems development structure.

Functions Analysis

The input data for functions analysis is the information gained from the identification and characterization of learning tasks. The purpose of functions analysis is to identify everything that has to be done by the system in order to facilitate the attainment of the specified learning tasks. At this point the questions of "done by whom" or "by what" are purposely avoided. These questions should not be raised until we know exactly what functions have to be carried out in order to master the learning tasks. It is important to understand this, because we want to allow for free, unrestricted speculation about functions.

In designing the system there are four functions which need to be accomplished. They include the following:
1. Selecting and organizing the content.
2. Selecting and organizing the learning experiences.
3. Managing the learners.
4. Evaluating the learning and operating the system.

Selecting and Organizing the Content

In many subjects, we have an almost unlimited amount of content from which to select. In foreign languages, for

Figure 11

The Relationship of Design Strategies

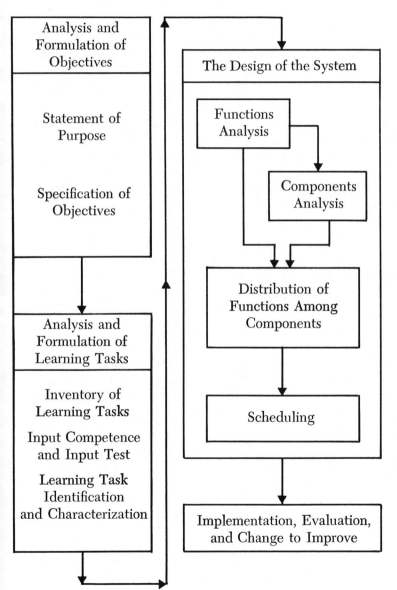

example, the vocabulary must be selected from thousands of available words. There are hundreds of basic situational contexts and numerous optional grammatical forms.

The selection of content, therefore, is a decision-making operation. As in any decision making, the aim should be to have an available rational basis upon which to select the content. As we have already mentioned, the characterization of learning tasks is a primary basis for selecting content. Information on the type of learning that a task represents helps to select appropriate content. But we should seek some other bases, too. In the foreign language field, for example, some of the factors that will influence content selection will include frequency of occurrence. Other considerations are the availability of an item, the flexibility of the item in saying different things with it, and learnability, which implies similarity, clarity, brevity, and regularity.[1] It should be noted, however, that the actual selection of course content is more complex than our neat example would suggest. In making a selection, we will find that some of the selection factors will be in conflict with others, for example, an item may occur frequently in the language, but not be easily learnable, or it may have a high degree of availability, but its coverage may be very limited.

In selecting content, the designer should consider the specific characteristics of the learning group and the individual differences of the learners. The content selected has to be relevant to the academic achievement and aptitude of the individual as well as to the span and type of interest of the student, his needs, his ability to handle abstractness or concreteness, and the specific level and style of his learning. This rationale points up the necessity of having available alternatives in content.

After the content has been selected it must be organized. The designer must decide what *follows* what content and what content *goes with* what content. The major strategies employed here will include sequencing, arrangement, and presentation.

There are two bases upon which to determine sequence. One is the type of learning a learning task represents and the other is the notion of a logical sequence. Characterization identifies the type of learning involved in certain learning tasks. The different types constitute a hierarchal arrangement. Within the domain of a subject matter, learning tasks that represent response learning should be pursued before tasks of the chain or multiple-discrimination type. The learning of specific concepts should precede the learning of any principle comprised of these concepts. Problem solving cannot be attempted until the principles that are to be used in the solution of the problem are discovered or mastered.

Within the realm of a specific kind of learning, tasks should be further ordered in a logical sequence. The designer should determine what should be known by the student in order for him to undertake the learning of this specific task. To help determine this information, a hierarchal structure of learning tasks can be constructed. This learning structure will tell us, for example, that the learning of task A is a prerequisite to the learning of task B and that the learning of task B is prerequisite to the learning of task C, and so on.

The *arrangement* of course content is a complex operation requiring the simultaneous weighting of the compatibility of content units and of the type and amount of learning that a selected content requires. For decisions about the type and amount, our guide is the information about conditions of learning and degree of difficulty that has already been discussed under the characterization of learning tasks.

Presentation is the final strategy of content organization. During this operation the content selected as a result of the strategies described above will be integrated into specific learning sequences of specific learning units and presented for the next strategy of instructional systems development.

Selecting and Organizing the Learning Experiences

The result of the content selection and organization will tell us what the learner is supposed to learn and in what sequence. It does not, however, tell us how this learning should take place. There are many alternatives for presenting the selected and organized content to the learner, just as there are many different ways of practicing, manipulating, and making use of content.

Implementing the strategies of the selection and organization of content, the significance of providing for alternatives in content in order to accommodate both individual and group has already been mentioned. In making design decisions about learning experiences, it is probably even more important to consider these differences. In regard to the processes of selection and organization of learning experiences, we should plan to have as many alternatives available as we need in order to cope with the great variations in the way people learn. Variation in the time needed to master a specific learning task is only one of the manifestations of individual differences. There are also differences in interest, need, aptitude, and achievement. Other aspects of individual differences include differences in the warm-up period needed, differences in ability to deal with abstractness or concreteness, differences in the interest span, and differences in sensory modes, such as audio or visual perception. There are also differences in the degree to which a person needs to be guided and in the amount of practice he requires. There are differences in the degree to which individuals are able to deal with complexities, work with and manipulate objects, equipment, machines, and so on. Furthermore, there are differences among individuals in the degree to which their imaginations can be involved, their creativity motivated, and to which they are able to solve problems. One of the most complex tasks of the designers of a system for learning is to identify or predict the expected effectiveness of each type of learning experience in relation to different types of learners. The designer needs to make assumptions about configurations and circumstances according to which specific types of learners will best accomplish certain learning tasks.

In selecting and organizing learning experiences, therefore, we have to deal with several variables. To start with, we need information on what the learner already knows that will help him master the learning tasks specified by our system. We should also have information on the aptitude variables and the learning style of the learner. We also need sets of alternative sets of learning experiences available from which to select those that will best match the abilities of the learner. Finally, we must formulate criteria for matching appropriate learning experiences to appropriate students.

While constructing his system, the designer is often tempted to speculate about what would be the best means and resources to use to carry out specific learning experiences. This inclination to reach ahead is indeed tolerated by the systems approach; in fact it is the recognition of the interdependence of method and media decisions that makes the systems approach particularly useful. Although the systems approach offers a specific structure for instructional decision making, this structure is not rigid. It has a built-in flexibility that enables the designer to think ahead. It is not a one-directional structure, but one which allows not only feedback, but also "feed-ahead" or "feed-forward." Strategies of the system approach and products of the strategies are to be continuously interrelated back and forth so that their interaction and mutual influence can be properly assessed. Whenever decisions are made about learning experiences, the designer of an instructional system has to trace back the expected outcome of the selected experience through content to learning tasks, input, and the specification of objectives. This feedback enables us to examine whether the selected learning experience best ensures conditions for the learning of the selected content, whether the selected content best accommodates mastering the learning task, whether the acquisition of the selected learning task provides for the needed capabilities or for the performance of the behavior described in the objectives. At the same time the designer will also think ahead and make predictions about the feasibility of the selected experience in terms of the components to be used in carrying out the scheduling and implementation of the system.

Managing the Learners

Previously we considered the selection and organization of content and the selection and organization of learning experiences. We shall now examine the third major aspect of functions analysis, the management of learners. The management of learners was described by Smith,[2] as the process of identifying and carrying out those functions that will keep the student productively participating in the learning activity. How then can the system best involve the learner and keep him interested in learning?

In developing a design for the management of learners, we need adequate data about the learner in order to introduce short-term and long-term incentives and to meet the requirements of the learner's uniqueness so that we can keep him optimally involved in learning. The management of learners will also include the designing of procedures and strategies whereby the teacher will have an appropriate selection of available curriculum alternatives.

Evaluation

This function provides for the constant monitoring of the learning and of the system. It poses an ongoing inquiry into the achievement of the learner and into the effectiveness and efficiency of the system. More specifically, the designer of the system must find answers to the following questions: On the basis of the progress he is making now, is the learner likely to attain his terminal objectives? If not, what adjustments need to be made? Are the functions provided by the

---

[2]Robert G. Smith, Jr., *The Design of Instructional Systems.* Technical Report 66-18 (Alexandria, Va.: HumRRO, 1966).

system the best ones to achieve system goals? What are some of the shortcomings? Where and how can it be improved? By pursuing these inquiries, we can monitor the learner and the system continuously.

The four strategies explored above comprise *functions analysis*. The curriculum resulting from functions analysis needs to be further qualified by the findings of *component analysis* which we will discuss in the following section.

Component Analysis

One of the most radical departures from present curriculum practices suggested by the systems approach is the way the designer of an instructional system makes decisions about the selection of the components of the system. The term *components analysis* refers to who or what should be employed to carry out the specific functions identified as the outcome of functions analysis.

Educators have rather firmly set ways of thinking about the employment of educational resources—men, media, and other material resources. We say the teacher is "in charge," inasmuch as he is in the classroom, is the students' main source of information, governs student behavior, and tests student achievement. He, of course, can use "aids" such as textbooks, and audiovisuals. This teacher-and-instruction centeredness has not changed much, even though nowadays we employ more and more teaching aids. With the help of NDEA funds we have purchased during recent years "half-price" equipment and media. So we have acquired lots of gadgets, even though we don't always know just what to do with them. Thus, we know of administrators who have gotten headaches from worrying about how to utilize their 60-booth modern remote-controlled beautiful language lab. (Have you ever heard about language lab cemeteries?)

The application of the systems concept to education has introduced a kind of thinking that is radically different from that described above. Systems thinking in education has brought about a new way of looking at the whos and whats of learning environment. More specifically, the value system expressed by and inherent in the term *teaching aids* has completely changed. We no longer talk about the teacher and his instructional aids, but about the components of a system that are considered and used on the basis of their ability to accomplish specific educational functions. This last statement is the central concept of component analysis.

Given a specific function, identified as the outcome of functions analysis, in the course of component analysis our problem is first to line up alternative means or components which have the potential required for carrying out the particular function in question and then, select from among these alternatives the one which appears to be the best to perform the function for which it is to be used. The system designer will choose the human resource, means, or tools that will best carry out the function and optimize the attainment of the predetermined performance. In conducting components analysis, system designers should never take a component for granted merely because it has been always used. On the other hand, they should not reject a component just because it has been used for a long time. One of the rules of component analysis is that the component should fit the function and not the function the component. The idea of function fitting the component, or the nonsystems way of thinking, is reflected in the widespread practice of assigning instructional functions to the teacher simply because he is in the classroom anyway. It is to overcome the temptation inherent in this habit that we insist on the order of identifying functions first and components next.

Another rule of components analysis is that the designer should always consider alternatives. In considering and surveying components we need to have the freedom to look for the one that offers the best possible potential to carry out the function and to select the one that is the most relevant to the learner. Next to best potential and relevancy, however, there are some other criteria to consider, such as practicality and economy. Because of these factors the designer should select the best component from the various alternatives after he has considered the limitations and constraints inherent in the system environment. Because of these considerations, the final decisions will not be made until the functions are actually distributed among the components. Distribution will be discussed later.

In surveying components, then, system thinking requires of us to keep in mind all the possible human and material resources relevant to and potentially capable of the accomplishment of specified functions. A component or a set of components should be selected on the basis of such criteria as (1) potential to accomplish a particular function, (2) ability to integrate with other components, (3) relevancy to the learner, (4) practicality, and (5) economy.

The human component will include the learner and the teacher, as well as personnel engaged in a wide variety of educational support and service functions. The material components will include both software and hardware, such as textbooks, programmed instructional materials, tapes, films, teaching machines, and other media.

Examples of Component Analysis

Let us now consider the teacher as a component of an instructional system. Extensive research done during recent years on the use of programmed materials has demonstrated that students can acquire information as well without the personal intercession of the teacher as they can with it.[3] We thus wonder about the role of the teacher as the source of information. A systematic component analysis will lead us to recognize that the teacher may be best described as being the manager of learning. This primary function may include providing for the motivation of the learner, for the planning and managing of learning experiences, and for the examining and exploiting—with the student—of the information the student has acquired.

[3] Winslow R. Hatch, "Approach to Teaching" (Washington, D.C.: Government Printing Office, 1966).

Some examples and hints about component selection will further clarify the appropriate use of this strategy. Going back to our language learning example, and having the improvement of the student's pronunciation in mind,[4] from the systems point of view one of the questions we can ask is, How can the function of the learning of sound production be facilitated by a designed interaction of man and media? This type of question is in rather sharp contrast to questions we usually ask, such as: How can the tape recorder and other media be used to aid the instructor in teaching pronunciation? The first question—the inquiry about designed interaction—would lead us to a different set of answers from the second; and it is these different kinds of answers that we seek through the use of the systems approach.

More specifically, when teaching pronunciation in the conventional way, usually the teacher demonstrates the sound and requires the student to copy the model. He may also use recorded utterances for this purpose. If the student has difficulty, the teacher might, if he has appropriate training, furnish information about the articulatory motions that the student should make.

In contrast to this, how would a teacher, who is familiar with the systems approach, proceed in designing student-teacher and student-media interaction for learning pronunciation? First, he will clarify the functions that pertain to facilitating the learning of a particular sound or utterance. These functions include (1) the presentation of the model, (2) information about the articulatory motions the student needs to make (3) feedback on correctness of pronunciation and aritculation. Considering the presentation of the model, next to the obvious authenticity, it will be required that the model be consistent and that the production of the sound be visibly observable by the student. What components can best satisfy these requirements? Possible alternatives include the teacher, a native informant, recorded speech, and visual pre-

[4]Bela H. Banathy, "The Systems Approach," *Modern Language Journal,* Vol. VI, No. 5, May 1967, pp. 281–89.

sentation of the image of the speaker. Except for consistency, the teacher with native speaker competence would be our first choice. The requirement of consistency calls for the recorded speech of the native speaker. To satisfy the requirement of visual presentation of the speaker, the recorded sound should be coupled with a visual display of the speaker. Therefore, if the teacher is a native speaker of the language, the optimum solution is to integrate his presentation with recorded sound and video images. If the teacher does not possess native competence, the recorded sound feature and the visual image of the speaker should be displayed for the student on a terminal.

Information on articulatory motions can be provided by the teacher through an explanation, by drawing articulatory diagrams on the board, or by using articulatory charts (stationary or animated). The visual representation of articulatory motions can also be projected on the screen of the student's terminal, combined with the image of the speaker as he pronounces the utterance and synchronized with the audio presentation of the sound feature. For feedback on accuracy of pronunciation, components may include the teacher, the student who records his own utterance and compares it with the recorded model, or a computer-based comparison with the model and automatic display of instructions for correction. The accuracy of facial movements of articulations can be observed and fedback by the teacher, or it can be accomplished by the student who, with the aid of a mirror, can observe his own facial movements and compare them with the visually displayed model.

The optimum environment for presenting pronunciation models appears to be a learning laboratory in which numerous components are available and in which the teacher arranges student-teacher and student-media interactions to facilitate the pronunciation competence of the student.

In conducting component analysis, the designer of a system for learning will first identify the functions that need to be carried out. Next he will assess the capabilities required to carry out these functions. Then he will consider alternative means which appear to possess needed capabilities. Finally, he will try out or test different combinations in order to seek out an optimum component design.

As an example of the assessment of the potential of a specific medium, we shall draw upon the Instructional Television Research Report of the U.S. Naval Training Device Center.[5] The report describes a set of criteria by which systematic judgment can be made as to the use of TV as a component.

1. For presentation or demonstration, television is applicable. For practice, it is not.

2. If two-way communication between instructor and student is necessary, television is not suitable. [Both of these criteria reflect the fact that television is a medium for presentation.]

3. If rapid dissemination of information, reaching many men early in training, or rapid distribution of new information is necessary or urgent, television is favored. Otherwise, television may be considered optional.

4. If there is a shortage of qualified instructors, television is favored. If not, television is optional.

5. If the training situation involves physical risk or danger, television is favored. If not, it is optional.

6. If training aids or actual equipment is in short supply, television is favored. If supplies are ample, television is optional.

7. If training aids and equipment are difficult to move because they are large, heavy, or unwieldy, this circumstance favors television. If they are easily moved, television is optional.

8. If closeups are necessary in viewing training, this is a plus factor for television.

9. If color is an essential element of the presentation, color television is required. Otherwise, black and white can be used.

10. If much training time is lost in moving from one training area to another, television is desirable. Otherwise, it is optional.

[5]U.S. Naval Training Device Center, "Instructional Television Research Reports," Human Engineering Report 20-TV-4, June 1956.

11. If making a sound record is very desirable, television can be used to prepare tapes or kinescopes. If the sound record is not important, television is optional.

12. If weather interferes with presentation, use of television can solve this difficulty.

Components of a learning system are selected on the basis of an evaluation of their capability to accomplish functions required for the mastering of learning tasks. The examples described above demonstrate the assessment of the potential of a specific component in a particular setting.

Component Analysis in Selecting and Organizing Content and Learning Experiences

The content of a course is usually determined by the selection of textbooks or series of books. Those who make these selections are usually state and local educational authorities, school or departmental committees, or—on the higher levels of education—the individual teacher. For all practical purposes, the learner is excluded from any participation in these functions. The selection and organization of learning experiences are often taken care of by simply following the textbooks. At best they are organized by the teacher with the occasional involvement of his class. The individual learner is seldom, if ever, considered as a valid component in the accomplishment of these functions.

During recent years there has been an increasing recognition of the need to provide for individual differences by having available curriculum alternatives. It has been suggested that variations in initial competence, in aptitude, and in rate and style of learning should be met by variations in content and learning experiences. The components used to determine what alternatives to choose, however, are usually people other than the student himself. It is the teacher who manages the instructional strategy. The counselor plays a role in gathering data on the student's achievement, background, interests, and needs. In the most advanced instructional setups, a computer may monitor the student's learning and prescribe, from available alternatives, the specific path to follow. Thus, in the contemporary educational scene, although there is greater emphasis on learning, the learner is not yet activated as a decision-making component. It is suggested that even the most "modern" practices can be regarded as only halfway measures.

In a system that grows around *learning*, components will be selected on the basis of their capabilities to best attend specific functions that need to be carried out in order to ensure the mastering of learning tasks. One of the key criteria in this learning-oriented system is to have a number of alternatives available, both in content and in learning experiences. These alternatives should be designed for the purpose of meeting individual differences. Another key criterion is that, in congruence with a learning-focused system, the learner be considered a primary component in making decisions about the selection and organization of content and learning experiences. These decisions should be made *with* him, rather than *for* him.

But how can we implement such learning and learner-oriented component selection? In selecting content, the designer will provide for alternative sets of content items which are aimed at the attainment of learning tasks. Alternatives will relate to potential individual differences and, thus, provide for variations in levels of sophistication or abstraction, degrees of complexity, gradedness, length, extent of coverage, and topics of interest. These alternatives will not be prescribed for the learner, but the learner will be used as a component for selecting the one most appropriate for him. He, himself, should have an opportunity to test the alternatives in order to find out which one he can best respond to or which stimulates him the most. It is also possible that the learner can come up with a new alternative, one unique to him. In order to do this, he needs to have data about himself. He will probably need the cooperation of his teacher, counselor, fellow students, or others in his environment. He will coordinate his decision making with that of others in order to make the best possible selection. If a computer is available, the student may feed it appropriate data about his previous achievement, his background, interests, abilities, and learning style. The computer can then give him clues he can use in designing his program.

The organization of his time is also subject to decisions by the learner. Likewise, the point at which he will enter the learning system will also depend on the measured (preferably self-assessed) input competence of the learner.

When it comes to the selection and organization of learning experiences, the role of the learner as a component in the accomplishment of these functions will probably significantly increase. Variations in the design of learning experiences will naturally be even greater than variations in the design of content. What all this will lead to is a system in which the learner will assume increasingly more responsibility for his learning; one in which he himself can and will generate the force needed for his own involvement.

The foregoing discussion and examples have described the process whereby we can conduct a component analysis. As an outcome of components analysis, the designer of a system will have available to him a set of alternative components. This information, together with the products of functions analysis, will become the basis for *distribution,* a topic we will discuss in the following section.

Distribution

Having identified functions and surveyed components, the designer of a system must assign specific functions to specific components. This process is called distribution. During the distribution of functions to components, the designer must consider what component offers the best potential to accomplish a particular function. He must also consider the constraints and limitations of the system. This analysis must be conducted for each component. Sometimes he will find that the most effective component is also the most expensive one and the outlay of money and excessive time involved may therefore require him to make some trade-offs and select instead a component that is still within the range of projected effectiveness and also within the cost limits of the system. The aspect that cannot be compromised or traded off, however, is the attainment of objectives. Proper distribution, therefore, will ensure the selection of components that will produce the predetermined output product and still be within the limitations and capabilities of the system. Briefly, the goal is to bring about the best possible output within the least possible time and at the lowest possible cost. Figure 12 illustrates the trade-off concept.

In Figure 12 two continuums are projected on the diagram, one to represent effectiveness and the other to represent cost. We cannot move below point A on the effectiveness continuum. If we did, the quality of the output would not be acceptable. On the other hand, we cannot move above point B on the cost continuum because we cannot afford it. These points are determined by the resources available to us. Arrows C and D indicate the direction of the most desired state. The purpose of the trade-off strategy is to attain the best possible output quality with the lowest possible expenditure.

Distribution is the stress point in the systems development process. It is at this point that key decisions are made and alternative functions and components are considered, weighed, and then rejected or selected. In view of the critical nature of this process, some further clarification is in order.

First, we must reemphasize that in making design decisions, *function* always leads and *component* always follows. By now this must sound logical to the reader, but making design decisions with this logic is not always easy. In order to exercise this logic we need to overcome the habit of some of our present practices. One of the marks of prevailing practices in education is that it is component oriented. Usually we first consider what components we already have

Figure 12

Trade-off Diagram

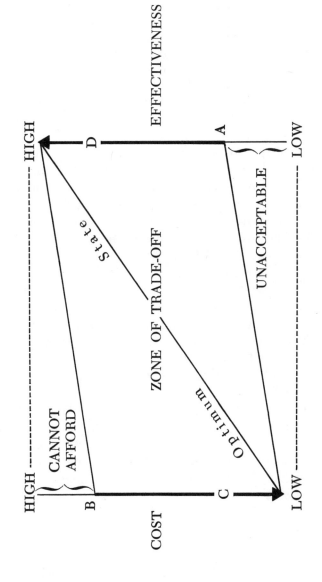

available—such as the teacher in the classroom and other resources, or whatever we can get at the market on the best terms, such as new textbooks and media—and then we assign functions to them. To break away from this way of thinking and to consider functions first is one of the crucial challenges in establishing a systems way of making design decisions in education.

The second point of clarification here is that most of the design decisions are made at the time the functions are distributed to the components. Consequently, the process and product of this strategy—distribution—will be most frequently reviewed during the operation of the system. Whenever feedback from output testing data, operational efficiency, or economy indicate a less than desirable product or state, we must reexamine the distribution, reanalyze the decisions we made, and identify points where adjustments may be in order. If systems objectives are not attained, the most likely area to find clues for introducing changes is distribution. If the system does not operate smoothly or if its economy is questioned, our distribution decisions are the first thing to reconsider. It is for these reasons that designers of systems have to keep detailed records of their design decisions, including a list of the alternatives considered, their characteristics, and an explanation for the decisions that were ultimately made.

There is also another system strategy—scheduling—which involves decision making. We will examine it in the following section.

Scheduling

Scheduling is that part of the learning system that is concerned with time and place. Once the distribution has been determined, we know what functions will be accomplished by what components. The designer must then decide when and where each function should take place. Scheduling places the information gained from distribution into a time-

and-place frame, thereby ensuring that human components and material resources with needed characteristics will be available at the appropriate time and at the place required for the purpose of carrying out functions in the most effective and economical manner.

The Nature of Strategies

In this chapter we have discussed the strategies of designing a system for learning. Reviewing these strategies, we may realize that their nature is of two kinds: analysis and synthesis. We can observe, however, a change in emphasis. During the phase of formulating objectives and learning tasks, which we covered in Chapters 3 and 4, we used analysis most intensively. The nature of the strategies described in this chapter, however, is more that of synthesis. There is also another important generalization we can make: Although we followed a sequence, one suggested by the over-all design structure, we have discovered that the process implied by these strategies is not linear. System designing is not a one-way street. The traffic is not a one-directional flow from objectives to tasks to functions to components, and so on. On the contrary, we need continuous regressive and progressive comparison, checking, adjusting, rechecking, and readjusting in order to achieve an adequate integration of the system. As a result of these processes the system becomes arranged into an organized, functional, and productive entity. These processes also best manifest the true nature and capability of systems development.

Implementation and Quality Control 6

The product of the processes of design and development is a system ready to be put into operation. Before the system is installed, however, two additional strategies should be introduced. One is called system training and the other, system testing.

System Training

System training is a preinstallation exercise of the system.[1] It helps to refine the operational interrelationship and the integration of the components or subsystems. During this dry run we can also ascertain if the components of the system really possess the needed capabilities. If deficiencies are discovered, we can introduce a training or adjustment process by which the required competence can be attained. At this point the two preinstallation strategies—training and testing—may complement each other. That is, any inadequacies or weak points in components or functions uncovered by system testing of components or strategies that are conducive to adjustment.

System Testing

The application of the systems concept also requires that we test the system before we install it. System testing serves the purpose of ascertaining whether or not the system can perform the processes for which it was designed. There are several ways to conduct system testing or system evaluation. As a minimum requirement the designer must think through the subsequent steps of the design process, continuously asking himself if the product of the particular step he is testing is the best one to achieve the objectives of the system. This thinking-through process can be done more formally by a systems analyst; in fact, it is advantageous that system testing be conducted by someone other than the designer. We can also set up a system simulation to demonstrate and evaluate the functioning of the system that we are designing.

A sophisticated approach to system simulation is to use computers. The use of computers, however, is limited to the testing of components or strategies that are conducive for

[1]Robert M. Gagné, *Psychological Principles in System Development* (New York: Holt, Rinehart and Winston, 1962).

quantification. This requirement places limitations on use of computers in this area.

In my view, the only satisfactory way to test an instructional system is by actually trying it out with students in the actual environment, or at least in a simulated environment. However, because system testing, or system evaluation, is an ongoing process, it is difficult to conclude that we have ever completed the testing. The best we can say is that we have probably done sufficient preinstallation testing and have made any needed corrections.

System Installation

System training and system testing are the two initial strategies of the implementation phase of systems operation. The product of these two strategies is the decision either to eliminate the system or to install it. If installation is decided upon, then the system is put into operation in its planned environment and it begins to process the input and then produce output. During operation, the system is continuously evaluated in order to measure its adequacy and the cumulative and terminal performance of the learner. Strategies of this evaluation will be discussed in the following section.

Evaluation and Quality Control

The purpose of evaluation and quality control is to ensure that the objectives of the system are being met or, if not, that adjustments will be introduced in order to correct the system so that objectives can be eventually attained. This phase of systems development is comprised of several strategies with specific purposes of their own, such as system monitoring, which is used to evaluate continuously the effectiveness of the system, and performance testing, which is a means of measuring the progressive achievement and terminal proficiency of the learner.

The continued accomplishment of these two strategies provides us with information we can use to carry out appropriate adjustments in order to improve the terminal performance of the learner and to optimize the effectiveness and economy of the system.

System Monitoring

Monitoring the system requires its continuous evaluation and analysis. The outcome of these operations informs us about the adequacy of the system. As the system operates, the designer must introduce such queries as

Are objectives clearly stated and formulated along measurable and operational lines?

Does the criterion test truly reflect the objectives?

Have we interpreted our objectives properly in exploring the learning tasks?

Have we properly assessed and tested input competence?

Do the learning tasks identify everything that has to be learned in order to enable the learner to perform in the way described by the objectives of the system?

Were any tasks identified that do not contribute to the attainment of the objectives?

Did we designate all functions needed to accomplish the learning tasks, or do we have some superfluous functions?

Have we selected the best possible and most economical components and are they functioning effectively?

Inquiries of this kind should also be used to explore distribution, scheduling, and system training and testing. As a result of these inquiries, we will be able to determine what changes, if any, are necessary to maintain or improve the quality of the product and the efficiency of the system. For example:

What operations or performance aspects of the system should be eliminated because they produce superfluously or serve something other than the stated system goals?

What operational and system performance aspects are lacking or are deficient and, thus, make less than their appropriate contribution to the system objectives?

Are we getting our money's worth? Can we improve the economy, and if so, how?

Performance Testing

The evaluation of the learner's performance is accomplished through continuous checking of student progress and by testing his performance capabilities at the terminal point.

Tests, which are used throughout the program, are designed for the purposes of

Measuring the input competence of the learner in relaton to the learning tasks to be attended.

Measuring the degree to which the learner has the competences that are prerequisite to mastering learning tasks.

Diagnosing learning style and learning rate so as to best accommodate the individual learner.

Assessing the progress of the learner in order to introduce changes that will enable him to perform in the expected way.

Pointing toward specific deficiences in the system itself.

The test that is to measure output performance should assess the degree to which the student is able to exhibit the behavior specified by objectives.

System Adjustments: Change to Improve

Existing educational programs do provide for the measurement of student progress and terminal proficiency. Test results are usually communicated to students to inform them of their progress and achievement. Test results, however, are only seldom used by design for the changing of the instructional program. One of the most salient aspects of the systems approach is the continuous feedback of performance data into the system for the purpose of making adequate adjustments in the system.

The self-adjusting characteristics of systems development prescribe change as a perpetual process in the development, operation, and maintenance of systems. We can safely say that the only valid means of maintaining a system is by purposely changing it. For those of us in education this characteristic of systems development is probably the most difficult to get used to.

Conclusion

The purpose of this study has been to explain and demonstrate the use of the systems approach in the development of instructional systems. The developmental design described here has presented us a structure and a set of strategies for making curriculum decisions.

The *nucleus* of a system for learning is its *purpose*. It is *purpose* from which *system objectives* can be derived. Based on objectives the designer has to determine whatever has to be learned in order to ensure the attainment of objectives. Next, *input competence* of the learner can be assessed in order to see if he has already acquired capabilities that are relevant to his learning task. The differential analysis of learning task as opposed to input competence provides a set of actual *learning tasks.*

Once we have identified and characterized the learning task, we can begin to design the system. We must consider functions that have to be carried out by the system to ensure the mastering of learning tasks. Next, functions have to be distributed among components. Decisions made on this basis lead to the design of the system. Following the *testing* and *training* of the system, its *installation* may proceed. Finally, the *feedback* gained from *output testing* and system monitoring is used to introduce adjustments and improvements in the system. Figure 13 summarizes the design of instructional systems.

Figure 13

The Design of Instructional Systems

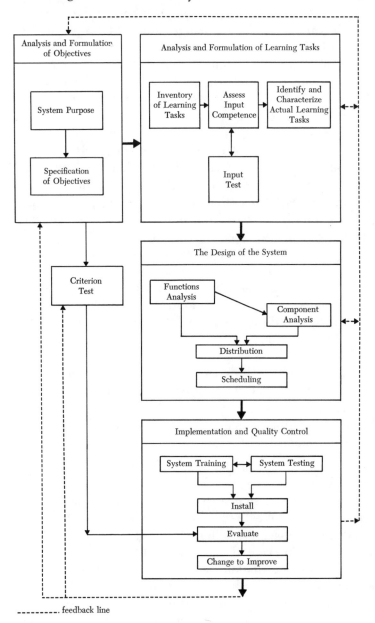

Innovation and Research

One of the most conspicuous characteristics of the systems approach is the necessity to change in order to improve the system. It is this characteristic and the feedback structure of the systems design that indicate that the systems approach has an inherent potential which, if properly explored, may offer a framework and a set of strategies for educational innovation and research.

In doing educational research, many of us have been frustrated by a demand to isolate variables and deal with them as single entities. We have faced this situation knowing that such a demand can seldom, if ever, be satisfied. In the contemporary educational setting, we have to accept the complexity of interacting variables and it is this phenomenon which the systems approach can best accommodate. The systems approach appears to make it possible to identify functions and components, describe their interaction, and then predict, observe, and measure the effect of change or variations in components and functions. The sequence of steps suggested by the decision-making structure outlined in this book suggests a sequence for exploring corruiculum innovation and research.

The application of the systems approach to the formulation of research strategies could have particular significance today when government, industry, and the educational establishment are putting increasingly more effort and funds into educational innovation and research.

Evaluation

A review of the design structure and strategies described in this book will indicate that the structure and strategies of the systems approach may offer a framework and procedures that are useful in evaluating existing curriculums. An analysis of an existing curriculum, a course of study, or an instructional unit will start out by inquiring into the purpose of the unit. What are the environmental demands, conditions, and constraints under which it is to function? Are objectives specified and formulated along measurable and operational lines? Does the performance test reflect these objectives? Is the input competence of the learner tested appropriately? Are learning tasks clearly identified and characterized? Can we locate content and learning experiences that do not actually serve the attainment of objectives? Have we provided for all that is needed to facilitate the expected performance? Do we have available adequate alternatives in content, learning experiences, and motivation? Do components demonstrate optimum capability in carrying out functions? These questions can also be applied to distribution, scheduling, implementation, and quality control. What is suggested here is that the inquiries which are pursued to develop a new system may also be introduced for the evaluation and analysis of existing programs. There are, of course, differences between the processes of analysis and evaluation of an existing system and that of building a new one. One of the differences is to pay full attention to specific systems constraints at the beginning of the analysis of an existing system, rather than, as we did in systems development, at the later stage during distribution. The other difference is implied by the term *analysis*. In evaluation, the nature of strategies used is analysis. We are not building a new system; we are only furnishing data that can be used to correct, adjust, or rebuild the system.

✻   ✻   ✻

Early in this discussion it was suggested that education is a system in the special sense implicit in the systems concept. Looking at education from a systems viewpoint, we have found that the systems approach appears to be a valid decision-making process for the design of educational systems.

In closing, I suggest that the message of this book is not limited to a description and demonstration of the educational use of systems development. I am convinced that the educational application of systems theory does more than offer decision-making and systems-development procedures. More specifically, I feel that the use of the systems concept in education provides a new insight into the purpose of education and puts a new emphasis on it. It forces us to face up to the question: What is education about? Once we have the answer to this question, then, and not until then, can we proceed to ask: What do we have to do about it? Systems thinking insists not only upon a clear statement of purpose, but also upon the logical and measured implementation of the purpose. I believe that if learning were taken seriously as its purpose, education would change from what it is today to something surely different. Having in mind the *learning* of specific skills, knowledge, and attitudes as the purpose of education will require us to make *learning* itself the key process after which the *learner* becomes the component around which all other components are organized.

The systems approach, thus, appears to have a dual role in education. First, as applied *in* education, it offers a powerful methodology for decision making and design development. Second, systems approach, as applied *to* education, may bring about a clear understanding of what education is truly about. It may be that it is from this second application that we will derive the greater benefit.

Glossary

ADJUSTMENT (of the system)

Process whereby the system is changed in order to improve the system output and/or to make the system more efficient and economical.

ANALYSIS OF LEARNING TASK

Process by which the designer of an instructional system identifies whatever the student has to learn in order to be able to perform the way described in the objective.

COMPONENT ANALYSIS

A process employed by the designer of a system in order to identify alternative human and material means that have the potential to carry out specific functions required for the attainment of system objectives.

COMPONENTS

Parts which comprise a system and which are selected to accomplish specific functions required for the attainment of the objectives of the system. (In education we have human components, such as the learner, teacher, counselor; media, such as books and audiovisual equipment; facilities, such as classrooms and playgrounds; and other material and financial means.)

CONSTRAINTS

Known limitations and restrictions in the capabilities of human and material resources involved in the design, development, and maintenance of a system.

CONTENT

As used in this book *content* has two meanings: (1) Its broader meaning implies the sum of all parts that make up a system; (2) content as an aspect of curriculum means elements of knowledge, skills, processes, and attitudes which are selected and organized and then presented through learning experiences to the student. The acquisition of content enables the student to perform the way described in the objectives.

CRITERION TEST
> The evaluation instrument employed to assess the degree to which the output performance of the student meets predetermined performance objectives.

DISTRIBUTION
> The process by which specific functions, required for the attainment of the purpose of the system, are assigned to selected components.

ENVIRONMENT (system)
> The larger context in which a system operates, from which it receives its purpose and resources and to which it is responsible for the use of resources and for the adequacy of its output. (For education, this larger context is the society.)

FEEDBACK
> A process built into a system by which output performance is compared with criterion performance and by which the information about the adequacy of the performance of the system and about the adequacy of its output is communicated to the designer and/or manager of the system.

FUNCTIONS
> Specific activities that need to be carried out in designing, developing, and maintaining a system in order to facilitate the attainment of the objectives of the system.

FUNCTIONS ANALYSIS
> The process by which the designer of a system identifies whatever is required to be done in order to ensure the attainment of objectives.

INPUT
> Whatever becomes subject to the system, or the material upon which the system operates.

INPUT COMPETENCE
> The capabilities of the input. In an instructional system, this term is usually used to denote the initial capabilities, knowledge, skills, and attitudes of the student.

INVENTORY OF LEARNING
> The listing of all that a person has to learn in order

to be able to perform in the way described in the performance objective.

LEARNING STRUCTURE

The logical, hierarchical arrangement of learning tasks.

LEARNING TASKS

Specific bits of knowledge, skills, and attitudes which the student has to master in order to be able to perform in the way described in the objective.

LIMITATION

Restrictions imposed upon the design, development, and management of a system by its environment.

MICRO-SYSTEM

A minimal designed entity built around a specified purpose for the attainment of which more than one function and more than one component are required. (In education, a micro-system can be envisioned as a brief lesson unit that can be completed in a few-to-several minutes, and is aimed at the attainment of a specified performance objective. It requires the selection and organization of specific content, method, personnel, and media, followed by scheduling, implementation, and the testing of output performance.)

OBJECTIVE

A statement that describes in observable and measurable terms the expected output performance of the product of the system.

OUTPUT

The product of a system; the result or outcome of processes employed by the system. (In education, the output is the student who has learned, or the knowledge that has been produced.)

OUTPUT PERFORMANCE

Performance relative to objectives, that the product of a system is able to exhibit at the terminal point.

PROCESS

The ongoing state of a designed entity manifested in doing whatever has to be done in order to attain the purpose of a system.

PURPOSE

The goal for which a system is designed; the nucleus around which a system grows. Usually, it is expressed as a broad and brief statement which informs us what the whole thing is about.

QUALITY CONTROL

The monitoring of a system and its planned change by which adjustments are introduced to correct for differences between actual output performance and performance expectations established by objectives.

SCHEDULING

The arrangements made to determine when and where a particular function of the system is to take place.

STRATEGIES

Components of the total process of systems design, development, and system management.

SUBSYSTEM

A part of a system, comprised of two or more components, with a purpose of its own and designed to interact with its peer subsystems in order to attain the over-all purpose of the system. (As an example, the instructional subsystem and the counseling and administrative subsystems interact by design, making up the system called the school.)

SUPRASYSTEM

A larger entity, designed for a specific purpose, which is comprised of two or more systems.

SYSTEM DEVELOPMENT

The endeavor of designing, from parts, entities as systems for the attainment of a specific purpose.

SYSTEM (MAN-MADE)

An entity comprised of parts which is designed and built by man into an organized whole for the attainment of a specific purpose.

SYSTEM TESTING

A pre-installation dry run of the system conducted in order to ascertain whether it can perform the operations for which it was designed.

SYSTEM TRAINING

A pre-installation exercise of the system carried out in order to refine functions, operational relationships, and the integration of components or subsystems.

SYSTEMS APPROACH

Common sense by design. A self-correcting and logical methodology of decision making to be used for the design and development of man-made entities. Component strategies of this methodology include the formulation of performance objectives, the analyses of functions and components, the distribution of functions among components, then scheduling, the training and testing of the system, installation, and quality control.

SYSTEMS VIEW

A way of thinking, by looking at man-made entities as systems, as assemblages of parts which are designed and built into an organized whole for the accomplishment of a specific purpose.

TASK LEVEL

A degree of specificity arrived at in formulating objectives according to which the expected performance is stated on the level of the smallest independent units of performance.

TRADE-OFF

The weighing of alternative means or components to be employed for the accomplishment of required functions with an intent to select the one that is the most economical and still offers the potential needed to ensure the attainment of objectives. The trade-off is between economy and effectiveness, having in mind not to spend more than what resources permit, but also not to compromise the attainment of objectives for the sake of economy.

Selected References

ACKOFF, L. RUSSELL, "Systems, Organizations and Interdisciplinary Research." In *Systems: Research and Design,* Donald P. Eckman (ed.), (New York: John Wiley & Sons, 1961).

————,*Scientific Method: Optimizing Applied Research Decisions* (New York: John Wiley & Sons, 1962).

ASMIOW, MORRIS, *Introduction to Design* (Englewood Cliffs, N.J.: Prentice-Hall, 1962).

BANATHY, BELA H., *Micro-Instructional Systems* (Monterey, Calif.: Project EDINN, Supplementary Educational Planning Center, 1968).

————, *A Theory of Selection and Organization of Content in Foreign Language Curricula.* Doctoral dissertation, University of California, Berkeley, 1966.

————, "The Systems Approach," *Modern Language Journal,* May 1967, pp. 281–289.

BANATHY, BELA H., and others, "The Use of Contrastive Data in Foreign Language Course Development." In *Trends in Language Teaching,* Albert Valdman (ed.), (New York: McGraw-Hill, 1966).

BARSON, JOHN, "Heuristics of Instructional Systems Development: A Team Report," *Audiovisual Instruction,* Vol. 12, No. 6, June–July 1967, pp. 613–614.

BARSON, JOHN, and EUGENE K. Oxhandler, "Systems: An Approach to Improving Instruction," *Audiovisual Instruction,* Vol. 10, No. 5, May 1965, p. 360.

BARSON, JOHN, JOHN M. GORDON, JR., and W. RUSSELL HORN-BAKER, "Standard Operating Procedures for a Learning Resources Center: A System for Producing Systems," *Audivisual Instruction,* May 1965, pp. 378–379.

BEYNON, ROBERT, "The Total Systems Concept: Research Implications," *Data Processing for Education* (Detroit:

American Data Processing, Inc., Vol. 5, No. 11, Dec. 1966.)
Paper read at the National Conference of State Educational
Information Systems, University of Iowa, Iowa City, May
1966.

BOULDING, KENNETH E., "General Systems as a Point of View."
In *Views on General Systems Theory,* Mihajlo D. Mesarovic (ed.), (New York: John Wiley & Sons, 1964).

BRICK, E. MICHAEL, "Learning Centers: The Key to Person-
alized Instruction," *Audiovisual Instruction,* Vol. 12, No. 8.
Oct. 1967, pp. 786–792.

BRIGGS, LESLIE J., "A Procedure for the Design of Multimedia
Instruction," *Audiovisual Instruction,* Vol. 12, No. 3, March
1967, pp. 228, 252.

BRIGHT, R. LOUIS, "Educational Technology as an Approach,"
Educational Technology, Jan. 15, 1968.

BROWN, JAMES W., "The Systems Solution to College Problems," *Educational Screen Audiovisual Guide,* Vol. 45, No.
5/457, May 1966.

BROWN, JAMES W., and JAMES W. THORNTON, JR. (eds.),
Newer Media in Higher Education (Washington, D.C.:
Association for Higher Education and the Division of
Audiovisual Instructional Service of the National Educa-
tion Association, 1963).

BROWN, THEODORE H., "Quality Control," In *New Decision-
Making Tools for Managers,* Edward C. Bursk and John
F. Chapman (eds.), (Cambridge, Mass.: Harvard Uni-
versity Press, 1963).

BULEY, HILTON C., "Multimedia Systems of Instruction,"
Audiovisual Instruction, Vol. 10, No. 5, May 1965, pp. 391–
392.

BUREAU OF NAVAL WEAPONS, SPECIAL PROJECTS OFFICE, *In-
struction Manual and Systems Procedures for the Program
Evaluation System (PERT)* (Washington, D.C.: Govt.
Printing Office).

BURNS, RICHARD W., "The Theory of Expressing Objectives,"
Educational Technology, Oct. 30, 1967.

BUSHNELL, DONALD D., "The Role of the Computer in Future
Instructional Systems," *AV Communication Review,* Vol.
11, No. 2, Supp. 7, March–April 1963.

————, "Computer Technology" Committee Print: *Notes and Working Papers Concerning the Administration of Programs*. Prepared for the Subcommittee on Education of the Senate Committee on Labor and Public Welfare (Washington, D.C.: Govt. Printing Office, 1967).

CANFIELD, ALBERT A., "A Rationale for Performance Objectives," *Audiovisual Instruction*, Feb. 1968.

————, "Instructional Systems Development," *Educational Screen and Audiovisual Guide*, June 1965.

CARR, C., and others, *Quantitative Decision Procedures* (New York: McGraw-Hill, 1964).

CARROLL, J. B., "School Learning Over the Long Haul." In *Learning and the Educational Process*, J. D. Krumboltz (ed.), (Chicago: Rand McNally, 1965).

CARTER, LAUNOR F., "Adapting Technology to Education," *Educational Technology*, Aug. 1966, pp. 9–12.

CARTER, LAUNOR F., and HARRY SILBERMAN, *The Systems Approach, Technology and the School*. U.S. Dept. of Commerce, Institute for Applied Technology, 1965.

CHAPANIS, A., "On Some Relations Between Human Engineering, Operations Research, and Systems Engineering." In *Systems: Research and Design*, Donald P. Eckman (ed.), (New York: John Wiley & Sons, 1961).

CHURCHMAN, C. W., "A Design for Systems Research on Instruction." Paper presented at the Conference on "New Dimensions for Research in Educational Media Implied by the 'Systems' Approach to Instruction," Center for Instructional Communications, Syracuse University, April 1964.

————, "An Approach to General Systems Theory." In *Views on General Systems Theory*, Mihajlo D. Mesarovic (ed.), (New York: John Wiley & Sons, 1964).

————, On the Design of Educational Systems," *Audiovisual Instruction*, Vol. 10, No. 4, May 1965, pp. 361–365.

CHURCHMAN, C. W., RUSSELL L. ACKOFF and E. LEONARD ARNOFF, *Introduction to Operations Research* (New York: John Wiley & Sons, 1957).

COGSWELL, JOHN F., *The System Approach as a Heuristic Method in Educational Development—An Application to the Counseling Function.* SP-270. (Santa Monica, Calif.: System Development Corp., March 1962).

―――――, "Systems Analysis and Computer Simulation in the Implementation of Media," *Audiovisual Instruction,* May 1965, pp. 384–386.

COGSWELL, JOHN F., and others, *Analysis of Instructional Systems.* Final Report. (Santa Monica, Calif.: System Development Corp., 1966).

COOK, D. L., "Applications of PERT to Education," Address presented at the PERT Workshop. Ohio State University, Columbus, Ohio, May 1965, p. 6.

CORRIGAN, ROBERT E., *The Group Tutorial System* (Los Angeles: Litton Instructional Materials, 1965).

―――――, *The Instructional Systems Approach to Tutorial Systems Development* (Anaheim, Calif: Litton Instructional Materials, 1965).

―――――, *Developing and Validating Instructional Materials Through the Instructional System Approach.* A paper presented at The National Conference on Systems Approaches to Curriculum and Instruction in the Open Door College. Los Angeles, University of California, July 1966 (Anaheim, Calif.: Litton Instructional Materials).

CORRIGAN, ROBERT E., and ROGER A. KAUFMAN, *Why System Engineering* (Palo Alto, Calif.: Fearon Publishers, 1965).

COULSON, JOHN E., "Technology and Educational Planning," *Educational Technology,* Feb. 28, 1968.

CRAWFORD, MEREDITH P., "Concepts of Training." In *Psychological Principles in System Development* (Robert M. Gagné (ed.), (New York: Holt, Rinehart & Winston, 1966) pp. 301–342.

DAVIS, ROBERT, "The Systems Concept in Education," *Educational Technology,* Vol. VII, No. 15, Aug. 1967, p. 3.

DAVIS, ROBERT, and RICHARD A. BEHAN, "Evaluating System Performance in Simulated Environments." In *Psychological Principles in System Development,* Robert M. Gagné (ed), (New York: Holt, Rinehart & Winston, 1966) pp. 477–516.

DEPARTMENT OF DEFENSE, OFFICE OF EDUCATION AND NSIA, *Education Systems for Education and Training.* Proceedings of Conference on above, June 1966.

DETERLINE, WILLIAM S., "The Secrets We Keep from Students," *Educational Technology,* Feb. 15, 1968.

ESBENSEN, THORWALD, *Working with Individualized Instruction; The Duluth Experience* (Palo Alto, Calif., Fearon Publishers, 1968).

ECKMAN, DONALD P. (ed.), *Systems: Research and Design.* Proceedings of the First Systems Symposium at Case Institute of Technology (New York: John Wiley & Sons, 1961).

EGBERT, R. L., and J. F. COGSWELL, "System Design in the Bassett High School." TM-1147, (Santa Monica, Calif.: Systems Development Corp., April 1963).

———— and ————, Systems Design for Continuous Progress School: Parts I & II (Santa Monica, Calif.: Systems Development Corp., 1964).

EISELE, JAMES E., "Computers in Curriculum Planning," *Educational Technology,* Nov. 30, 1967.

ELLIS, DAVID O., and FRED J. LUDWIG, *Systems Philosophy* (Englewood Cliffs, N.J.: Prentice-Hall, 1962.)

ELY, DONALD P., "Educational Technology as Instructional Communication," *Educational Technology,* Jan. 15, 1968.

ENTHOVEN, ALAIN, C., "The Systems Analysis Approach," *Planning-Programming-Budgeting.* Committee Print. Presentation prepared for the Special Subcommittee on the Utilization of Scientific Manpower, Senate Labor and Public Welfare Committee, 89th Congress, 2d Sess., May 1966.

FINAN, JOHN L., "The System Concept as a Principle of Methodological Decision." In *Psychological Principles in System Development,* Robert M. Gagné (ed.), (New York: Holt, Rinehart & Winston, 1966) pp. 517–546.

FINN, JAMES D., "AV Development and the Concept of Systems," *Teaching Tools,* Fall 1956.

————, "Technology and the Instructional Process," *Audiovisual Communication Review,* Vol. 8, No. 1, Winter 1960.

————, "A Possible Model for Considering the Use of Media in Higher Education," *Audiovisual Communication Review*, Vol. 15, No. 2, Summer 1967, pp 153–157.

————, "Educational Technology and Innovation." Committee Print, *Notes and Working Papers Concerning the Administration of Programs,* prepared for the Subcommittee on Education of the Senate Committee on Labor and Public Welfare (Washington, D.C.: Govt. Printing Office, 1967).

FINN, JAMES D., and others, *A Selective Bibliography on New Media and Instructional Technology,* Staff Paper No. 1, Instructional Technology and Media Project (Los Angeles: School of Education, University of Southern California, April 1964).

FLAGLE, CHARLES D., and WILLIAM H. HUGGINS, and ROBERT H. ROY (eds.), *Operations Research and Systems Engineering* (Baltimore: Johns Hopkins Press, 1960).

FLANAGAN, JOHN C., "Functional Education for the Seventies," *Phi Delta Kappan,* Vol. XLIX, No. 1., Sept. 1967, pp. 27–32.

FLOTHOW, RUDOLPH C., *The Selective Use of System Technology for Education, Conference Record,* 1967 Winter Convention on Aerospace and Electronic Systems, Vol. VI (Los Angeles, Feb. 1967).

GAGNÉ, R. M., *The Conditions of Learning* (New York: Holt, Rinehart & Winston, 1965).

————, "Educational Objectives and Human Performance." In *Learning and the Educational Process,* J. D. Krumboltz (ed.), (Chicago: Rand McNally, 1965) pp. 1–24.

————, "Human Functions in Systems." In *Psychological Principles in System Development,* Robert M. Gagné (ed.), (New York: Holt, Rinehart & Winston, 1966) pp. 35–74.

————, "Curriculum Research and the Promotion of Learning." In *Perspectives of Curriculum Evaluation,* B. Othanel Smith (ed.), (Chicago: Rand McNally, 1967) pp. 19–38.

———— (ed.), *Psychological Principles in System Development* (New York: Holt, Rinehart & Winston, 1966).

GENERAL ELECTRIC COMPUTER DEPARTMENTS, *Critical Path Method Program.* GE-200 Series. CD225k1.004. Rev. Nov. 1964. (Computer Dept., G.E. Co., Phoenix, Arizona.)

GENTILE, J. RONALD, "The First Generation of Computer-Assisted Instructional Systems: An Evaluative Review," *AV Communication Review*, Vol. 10, No. 2, March–April 1962, pp. 75–84.

GILPIN, JOHN, "Design and Evaluation of Instructional Systems," *Audiovisual Communication Review*, Vol. 10, No. 2, March–April 1962, pp. 75–84.

GLASER, ROBERT, "Educational Technology as Instructional Design," *Educational Technology*, Jan. 15, 1968.

———, "Psychological Bases for Instructional Design," *Audiovisual Communication Review*, Vol. 14, No. 4. Winter 1966, pp. 433–449.

———, "Implications of Training Research for Education." In *Theories of Learning and Instruction*, Ernest R. Hilgard (ed.), Sixty-Third Yearbook, NSSE (Chicago: University of Chicago Press, 1964).

———, "Components of the Instructional Process." In *Educational Technology*, J. P. DeCecco (ed.), (New York: Holt, Rinehart & Winston, 1964) pp. 68–76.

———, "Toward the New Pedagogy," *Educational Technology*, Spring 1967.

GOLDBERG, ALBERT L., "First Steps in the Systems Approach," *Audiovisual Instruction*, Vol. 10, No. 5, May 1965, pp. 382–383.

GUBA, EGON G., "Evaluation and the Process of Change," Committee Print: *Notes and Working Papers Concerning the Administration of Programs.* Prepared for the Subcommittee on Education of the Senate Committee on Labor and Public Welfare (Washington, D.C.: Govt. Printing Office, 1967).

HALE, ELIZABETH H., "PERT (Program Evaluating Review Technique), An ASTIA Report Bibliography" (Washington, D.C.: Office of Technical Services, Dept. of Commerce (AD-297-800), 1963).

HALL, A. D., and R. E. FAGEN, "Definition of a System," *General Systems,* Vol. 1, 1956.

HATCH, WINSLOW R., *Approach to Teaching* (Washington, D.C.: Govt. Printing Office, 1966).

HEDEGARD, JAMES M., "An Overview of Historical Formulations." In *Instruction, Some Contemporary Viewpoints,* Laurence Siegel (ed.), (San Francisco: Chandler, 1967).

HEINICH, ROBERT, "Educational Technology as Technology," *Educational Technology,* Jan. 15, 1968.

————, "The Systems Approach in Elementary and Secondary Education." Reviewed in *Audiovisual Instruction,* June-July 1966.

HERRMANN, CYRIL C., and JOHN F. MAGEE," 'Operations Research' for Management." In *New Decision-Making Tools for Managers,* Edward C. Bursk and John F. Chapman (eds.), (Cambridge, Mass: Harvard University Press, 1963).

HITCH, C. J., "On the Choice of Objectives in Systems Studies." In *Systems: Research and Design,* Donald P. Eckman (ed.), (New York: John Wiley & Sons, 1961).

————, "Decision-Making in Large Organizations," *Planning-Programming-Budgeting.* Committee Print, Royal Society Nuffield Lecture, London, England, Oct. 1966.

HUMPHREY, JOHN H., "Educational Technology—'Science of the Practical'," *Educational Technology,* Jan. 15, 1968.

KAIMANN, R. A., "Educators and PERT," *Journal of Educational Data Processing,* Spring 1966, p. 52.

KAPFER, PHILIP C., "An Instructional Management Strategy for Individualized Learning," *Phi Delta Kappan,* Vol. XLIX, Jan. 1968.

KAUFMANN, A., *Methods and Models of Operations Research* (Englewood Cliffs, N.J.: Prentice-Hall, 1963).

KENNEDY, JOHN L., "Psychology and System Development." In *Psychological Principles in System Development,* Robbert M. Gagné (ed.), (New York: Holt, Rinehart & Winston, 1966) pp. 13–34.

KEPPLE, FRANCIS, "Education's Age of Flexibility," *Educational Technology,* Vol. VII, No. 1, pp. 1–3.

KERSHAW, JOSEPH A., and ROLAND N. MCKEAN, *Systems Analysis and Education* (Santa Monica, Calif: Rand Corp., 1959).

KIRSHNER, R. B., "A Survey of Systems Engineering Tools and Techniques." In *Operations Research and Systems Engineering*, C. D. Flagle, W. H. Huggins, and R. H. Roy (eds.), (Baltimore: Johns Hopkins Press, 1960).

KNIRK, FREDERICK G., "Analysis of Instructional Systems: A Reaction," *Audiovisual Instruction*, Oct. 1965.

KOPSTEIN, FELIX F., *The Systems Approach to Education: An Introduction* (Princeton, N.J.: Educational Testing Service, 1966).

————, *General Systems Theory as the Basis for a Theory of Instruction*, Research Memorandum 66–8 (Princeton, N.J.: Educational Testing Service, July 1966).

LEHMANN, HENRY, *8 Steps in the Design of an Education and Training System.* Prepared by Task Group on the Systems Approach to Education and Training (Washington, D.C.: NSIA, Project Aristotle Symposium, Dec. 1967).

LIBSITZ, LAWRENCE (ed.), "Systems Approach Makes Progress," *Educational Technology*, July 1966, pp. 13–14.

LITTON INDUSTRIES, *New Path to Learning (The Systems Approach)*, 16mm color-sound film (Beverly Hills, Calif: Litton Industries).

LUMSDAINE, A. A., "Educational Technology, Programmed Learning, and Instructional Science." In *Theories of Learning and Instruction*, E. R. Hilgard (ed.), Sixty-Third Yearbook, NSSE (Chicago: University of Chicago Press, 1964).

MACCIA, GEORGE S., *An Educational Theory Model: General Systems Theory.* Bureau of Educational Research and Service, Occasional Paper 62–126 (Columbus: Ohio State University, Dec. 1962).

MACKEY, WILLIAM FRANCIS, *Language Teaching Analysis* (London: Longmans, Green & Co., 1965).

MAGER, ROBERT F., "Deriving Objectives for the High School Curriculum," *NSPI Journal (National Society for Programmed Instruction)*, March 1968.

————, *Developing Attitude Toward Learning* (Palo Alto, Calif.: Fearon Publishers, 1968).

————, *Preparing Instructional Objectives* (Palo Alto, Calif.: Fearon Publishers, 1962).

————, "The Instructional Technologist," *Educational Technology,* Vol. VII, No. 9. May 15, 1967, pp. 1–4.

MAGER, ROBERT F., and KENNETH N. BEACH, JR., *Developing Vocational Instruction* (Palo Alto, Calif.: Fearon Publishers, 1967).

MALCOLM, D. G., *Extensions and Applications of PERT as a System Management Tool.* Armed Forces Management Association, Seventh National Conference, Washington, D.C., Feb. 1961.

MAUCH, JAMES, "A Systems Analysis Approach to Education," *Phi Delta Kappan,* 43:158–162, June 1962.

MEALS, DONALD W., "Heuristic Models for Systems Planning," *Phi Delta Kappan,* Vol. XLVII, No. 5, Jan. 1967, pp. 199–203.

MESAROVIC, MIHAJLO D. (ed.), *Views on General Systems Theory* (New York: John Wiley & Sons, 1964).

MILLER, RICHARD I., "A Systems Approach," *Educational Screen and Audiovisual Guide,* Vol. 46, No. 10/471, Oct. 1967, pp. 28–29, 44.

MILLER, ROBERT B., "Task Description and Analysis." In *Psychological Principles in System Development,* Robert M. Gagné (ed.), (New York: Holt, Rinehart & Winston, 1966) pp. 187–228.

MILLER, ROBERT W., "How to Plan and Control with PERT." In *New Decision-Making Tools for Managers,* Edward C. Bursk and John F. Chapman (eds.), (Cambridge, Mass: Harvard University Press, 1963).

ODIORNE, GEORGE S., "A Systems Approach to Training," *Training Directors Journal,* Oct. 1965.

OPTNER, STANFORD L., *Systems Analysis for Business Management* (Englewood Cliffs, N.J.: Prentice-Hall, 1960).

————, *Systems Analysis* (Englewood Cliffs, N.J.: Prentice-Hall, 1964).

————, *Systems Analysis for Business and Industrial Problem Solving* (Englewood Cliffs, N.J.: Prentice-Hall, 1965).

O'TOOLE, JOHN F., JR., *Systems Analysis and Decision-Making in Education* (Santa Monica, Calif: Systems Development Corp., 1965).

OXHANDLER, EUGENE K., "Bringing the 'Dons' Up-To-Date." In *A New Look at an Old Educational System* (Syracuse: Audiovisual Center, Syracuse University, 1963). Paper delivered at the Dept. of AV Instruction, NEA Convention, Denver, April 1963).

――――, *New Systems for Education Suggested by Operations Research* (Syracuse: Center for Instructional Communications, The Newhouse Communications Center, Syracuse University, 1964). Paper delivered at Educational Communications Convocation, New York City, Nov. 1964.)

――――, "Afterthoughts on a Systems Conference," *Audiovisual Instruction*, May 1965, pp. 395–397.

PASK, GORDON, "Men, Machines and the Control of Learning," *Educational Technology*, Vol. VI, No. 22, Nov. 30, 1966, pp. 1–12.

PEARLMAN, JEROME, "Engineering Program Planning and Control Through the Use of PERT," *IRE Transaction on Engineering Management*, Vol. EM-8, No. 4, Dec. 1960, pp. 125-134.

POPHAM, JAMES W., and EVA L. BAKER, *Appropriate Practice. Educational Objectives. Establishing Performance Standards. Evaluation. Perceived Purpose. Selecting Appropriate Educational Objectives. Systematic Instructional Decision-Making.* A set of seven illustrated filmstrips with accompanying audio-taped narrations and instructional manual (Los Angeles: VIMCET Associates, 1967).

RAPOPORT, ANATOL, "In Search of Quantifiiable Parameters of Group Performance." In *Systems: Research and Design*, Donald P. Eckman (ed.), (New York: John Wiley & Sons, 1961).

――――, "Remarks on General Systems Theory." In *Views on General Systems Theory*, Mihajlo D. Mesarovic (ed.). (New York: John Wiley & Sons, 1964).

RATH, GUSTAVE J., "A Critique: Models, Means and Measurement in Education," *Educational Technology*, Jan. 30, 1968.

ROGERS, CARL R., "The Facilitation of Significant Learning." In *Instruction, Some Contemporary Viewpoints,* Laurence Siegel (ed.), (San Francisco: Chandler, 1967).

RYANS, DAVID G., *An Information Systems Approach to the Theory of Instruction with Special Reference to the Teacher* (Santa Monica, Calif.: Systems Development Corp. 1963).

————, "A Model of Instruction Based on Information Systems Concepts." In *Theories of Instruction,* Robert R. Leeper (ed.), (Washington, D.C.: Association of Supervision and Curriculum Development, NEA, 1965).

SCHURE, ALEXANDER, "Educational Escalation Through Systems Analysis," *Audiovisual Instruction,* Vol. 10, No. 5, May 1965, pp. 371–376.

SCRIVEN, MICHAEL, "The Methodology of Evaluation." In *Perspectives of Curriculum Evaluation,* B. Othanel Smith (ed.), (Chicago: Rand McNally, 1967), pp. 39–83.

SHELTER, RICHARD, "The Challenge of Educational Technology," *Educational Technology,* Spring 1967.

SIEGAL, LAURENCE (ed.), *Instruction, Some Contemporary Viewpoints* (San Francisco: Chandler, 1967).

SILVERMAN, ROBERT E., "Two Kinds of Technology," *Educational Technology,* Jan. 15, 1968.

SILVERN, LEONARD C., "A Cybernetic System Model for Occupational Education," *Educational Technology,* Jan. 30, 1968.

————, *Systems Engineering in the Educational Environment* (Hawthorne, Calif.: Northrop Corp., 1963).

————, *Fundamentals of Teaching Machine and Programmed Learning Systems* (Los Angeles: Education and Training Consultants, 1964).

————, "The Systems Aspect." In *Administrative Factors Guide* (Los Angeles: Education and Training Consultants Co., April 1964), pp. 16–22.

————, *Systems Engineering of Learning—Public Education K-12: Vol. 1. An Analysis; Vol. 2. A Synthesis* (Los Angeles: University of Southern California, 1965).

————, "Studies in the Systems Engineering of Education, I: Basic Data on the Evolution of Systems Thinking in Education." In *Instructional Technology and Media Project* (Los Angeles: School of Education, University of Southern California, 1965).

SILVERN, LEONARD C., and D. G. PERRIN, "Systems Engineering of Learning—The Training System." (Sound filmstrip.) (Los Angeles: Education and Training Consultants, April 1964).

SLACK, CHARLES W., "The Politics of Educational Objectives," *Educational Technology,* Vol. VII, No. 14, July 30, 1967, pp. 1–4.

SMITH, E. D., "The Use of PERT in Education." Proceedings of the Ninth College and University Machine Records Conference (Palo Alto, Calif: Educational Systems Corp., 1964).

SMITH, KARL U., and MARGARET F. SMITH, *Cybernetic Principles of Learning and Educational Design* (New York: Holt, Rinehart & Winston, 1966).

SMITH, ROBERT G., JR., *Controlling the Quality of Training.* Technical Report 65–6, June 1965. HumRRO, The George Washington University Human Resources Research Office (Dept. of the Army).

———, *The Design of Instructional Systems.* Technical Report 66–18, Nov. 1966. HumRRO, The George Washington University Human Resources Research Office (Dept. of the Army).

———, *The Development of Training Objectives.* Research Bulletin 11, June 1964. HumRRO, The George Washington University Human Resources Research Office (Dept. of the Army).

SOCIETY FOR GENERAL SYSTEMS RESEARCH, *General Systems.* Yearbook of the Society for General Systems Research, 1956–1967, Vols. I–XII. Bedford, Mass.

SPRINGER, C. H., "The 'Systems' Approach." *Changing Directions in American Education.* In *Saturday Review,* Jan. 14, 1967.

STAKE, ROBERT E., "Toward a Technology for the Evaluation of Educational Programs," *Perspectives of Curriculum Evaluation,* B. Othanel Smith (ed.), (Chicago: Rand McNally, 1967) pp. 1–12.

STEWART, DONALD K., "The Articulated Instructional Media Program at the University of Wisconsin," *Audiovisual Instruction*, May 1965, pp. 380–382.

————, *A Learning Systems Concept as Applied to Courses in Education and Training* (Pamphlet). (College Station, Texas: Center for Creative Application of Technology to Education.)

STOLUROW, LAWRENCE M., *Some Educational Problems and Prospects of a Systems Approach to Instruction*. Technical Report No. 2 (Urbana, Ill.: Training Research Laboratory, University of Illinois, March 1964).

————, *Systems Approach to Instruction*. Technical Report No. 7 (Urbana, Ill.: Training Research Laboratory, University of Illinois, July 1965).

————, "Model the Master Teacher or Master the Teaching Model." In *Learning and the Educational Process*, J. D. Krumboltz (ed.), (Chicago: Rand McNally, 1965).

SUPPES, PATRICK, "The Computer and Excellence," *Changing Directions in American Education*. In *Saturday Review*, Jan. 14, 1967.

TABA, HILDA, "Curriculum Development." In *Notes and Working Papers Concerning the Administration of Programs*. Committee Print Prepared for the Subcommittee on Education of the Senate Committee on Labor and Public Welfare (Washington, D.C.: Govt. Printing Office, April 1967).

TRACY, WILLIAM R., and others, "Systems Approach Gets Results," *Training in Business and Industry*, June 1967.

TROW, CLARK, "Behavioral Objectives in Education," *Educational Technology*, Dec. 30, 1967.

————, *Teacher and Technology, New Designs for Learning* (New York: Meredith Publishing Co., 1963).

TYLER, RALPH W., "Some Persistent Questions on the Defining of Objectives." In *Defining Educational Objectives*, C. M. Lindvall (ed.), (Pittsburgh: University of Pittsburgh Press, 1964).

————, "Evaluation—The Ultimate Reality," *Educational Technology*, Vol. VI, No. 18, Sept. 30, 1966, pp. 12–14.

————, "Changing Concepts of Educational Evaluation." In *Perspectives of Curriculum Evaluation,* B. Othanel Smith (ed.), (Chicago: Rand McNally, 1967) pp. 13–18.

UNWIN, DERICK, "Applying Educational Technology," *Educational Technology,* Jan. 15, 1968.

U.S. AIR FORCE, AIR FORCE SYSTEMS COMMAND, *Systems Management.* System Program Management Procedures, May 31, 1966.

VON BERTALANFFY, LUDWIG, "An Outline of General Systems Theory," *British Journal of Philosophical Science,* 1:148, 1950.

————, "General Systems Theory," *Main Currents in Modern Thought,* Vol. 71, 1955.

WALBESSER, HENRY H., *Constructing Behavioral Objectives* (College Park, Md.: College of Education, University of Maryland, 1968).

WORKING GROUP, WOODS HOLE CONFERENCE ON EDUCATION, *The Systems Approach to the Improvement of Education,* 1959. (Unpublished.)

WRIGHT, GEORGE O., *A General Procedure for Systems Study.* WADD Technical Note No. 60–18, Wright Air Development Division, Air Research and Development Command, Wright-Patterson AFB, Ohio, Jan. 1960.